UNLEASHING GENIUS

Leading Yourself, Teams and Corporations

by Paul David Walker

CEO Coach

Leadership Consultant

Poet

Philosopher

Morgan James Publishing • New York

UNLEASHING GENIUS

Library of Congress Control Number: 2007938787
Hardcover ISBN: 978-1-60037-340-4
Paperback ISBN: 978-1-60037-341-1

Published by:

www.morganjamespublishing.com

Morgan James Publishing, LLC
1225 Franklin Ave. Ste 325
Garden City, NY 11530-1693
Toll Free 800-485-4943
www.MorganJamesPublishing.com

Cover and Interior Design by:
Michelle Radomski
One to One Creative Services
www.creativeones.net

To my son, Janne Dylan Walker,
who is always working
to unleash his genius and the genius
of our family and his friends.

You are an inspiration to me.

ACKNOWLEDGEMENTS

There are many people who have helped me reach these understandings; other authors, each of my clients who I struggled with to build businesses, and mentors both named here and forgotten. I thank all who seek to make the world a better place to live now, and in the future, for our children.

Specifically, I would like to thank: My father, John Bruce Walker, for teaching me that nothing is impossible, and my mother, Marion Walker, for her constant support and love. I also thank my mentors and teachers: Dr. Ellsworth Barnard, Don Ross, Larry Senn, Linda and George Pransky, and Sydney Banks for their insight and support.

I would also like to thank JD Buckwell for his inspiration and courage. He insisted that I put these understandings in a book so that others can benefit from them.

Jerry Miller and Jon Winder who have taught me how to write and market a book are owed a debt of gratitude.

But, most of all, I want to thank my wife, Bonnie Joyce Walker, who has inspired me to unleash my genius when I thought it was not worthy of communication. I also want to thank her for being my editor, business manager, and partner all these years. It is rare that a husband and wife can work together on a commonly held vision, and I am grateful that we share the same vision for ourselves and the world.

TESTIMONIALS

Here is what people say
about Paul David Walker

"Rich, inspiring, soulful... One would almost think a poet wrote it!"

—Edward Rocky, PhD,
Professor of Business Administration, Pepperdine
University, Previously Dean of the School of Business

"Paul is—and has always been, since the day we first met— my Mentor. In that capacity, he is privy to my innermost thoughts. It is I who owes him a debt of gratitude that cannot be paid back in this lifetime."

—Ashwin Rangan, CIO of Wal-Mart.com

"Having worked closely with Paul Walker, I know how eminently qualified he is on the subject of leadership— giving him the unique ability to provide mentoring and coaching to those in a leadership position."

—Don H. Davis, Jr., Chairman of the Board and,
Chief Executive Officer Rockwell Automation

"Paul: I thoroughly enjoyed reading your chapter. I think it will make a very good book."

—Larry Allison, Editorial Editor, Press Telegram

"A realization that everything is connected invokes the obvious conclusion that operating from maximum consciousness instead of distorted cognitive thinking is the only point of being from which wisdom is fueled, instinct untainted by fear, paranoia, irrelevant variables and other "noise" can be achieved. Simple tools like self interruption, questions of the moment to discover the truth of what is already there, and unfiltered recognition of one's true current state (thus a chance to reset, calibrate, effectively return to consciousness) is truly liberating."

—Mike L. Chase, CCIE# 7226
Director, Cisco Advanced Technology Solutions (CATS)

"Paul's real value to the Chief Executive Officer of any business organization is that he understands the concept of how cultural change is necessary to develop real growth, working with managers to develop and implement change and provide concrete solutions.

Paul understands the concept of leadership and how it can affect an organization. I highly recommend his leadership approach to any company that needs to change its cultural organization or wants to provide exceptional leadership to meet both short and long term goals."

—Joseph F. Prevratil, President & CEO, RMS Foundation, Inc.

"I feel lighter and freed from a burden. My success as head of Inside Sales has grown considerably. I have been able to keep my mind clear, allowing me to focus on the challenges at hand without draining my energy.

I only mean to be sincere, not complimentary, when I say that reading your book has really made a difference. My life is better due to the insights you and your book have provided."
—Liz Arriola,
Inside Sales Manager, Rubbercraft Corporation

"I was especially impacted by the story of Don Ross, the CEO of New York Life, and his courageous action to follow his voice of wisdom and the lesson he taught you. I met with one of my CEO clients and had the opportunity to draw on that story to help him understand a key issue facing him and his company. It was a very powerful and impactful session."
—Norman S. Wolfe,
President/CEO, Quantum Leaders, Inc

"Because of your expertise we achieved objectives in an extremely timely fashion."
—Don Ross, Chairman and CEO, New York Life

"We took an enormous leap forward, making our words about a special company become a reality."
—Ken Simonds, CEO, Teradata

"We have come together as a team so that all energies are focused on our vision and mission."
—John Lee, President, ELC

"He is direct, insightful and not afraid to get in my face... key to my selection as CEO"
—Raouf Halim, CEO, MindSpeed Technologies

"He possesses a unique combination of business, teambuilding and executive development skills. I am sure many other CEOs, as I have, will benefit from his work"

—Dwight Decker,
Chairman and CEO, Conexant Systems Inc.

In an article in Symphony Magazine, John Forsyte, CEO of the Pacific Symphony, calls Paul David Walker's work "Invaluable." Walker, who has been coaching executives for 25 years, attends key meetings, meets with Forsyte regularly, and coaches him through encounters in advance. "Paul is coaching me on how to be a more empathic listener, and how to organize staff teams, things that are not necessarily intuitive to me."

—Symphony Magazine

"The meeting Paul facilitated with my team was the best meeting I have ever attended."

—Chris Lappi, CIO, ReMAE

"When Paul facilitates a meeting, he brings a stillness that seems to calm down the participants."

—Gerald Miller, City Manger, Long Beach

"Our Arrowhead off-site meeting was one of the most beneficial team-building exercises I have been involved with; my meeting with you, one-on-one, was also of great value not only to me, but to the entire Command Staff. We indeed have benefited by our relationship with you.'

—David W. Ellis, Fire Chief, City of Long Beach

Unleashing Genius
Foreword

With the birth of my two grandchildren this past year, I was reawakened to the beauty and innocence of children, especially newborns, but certainly true of all children. Children are special. We have a natural tendency to focus on their innocence. As I write this foreword, I cannot but think of their genius as well. What will they be and how will they contribute to this wonderful world we live in. What will they do with their lives? The world is before them. How will they use it? What is their genius? Of course it is too early to tell, and yet I know that they have their own personal genius and it will come to light soon enough. I hope it is sooner rather than later, so that they and all the world can see and benefit from what they offer as participants on the planet. As they grow up, it is my fondest wish to be able to help them to unleash their genius the way Paul has helped me to unleash mine.

When Paul asked me to write this foreword, I was honored and excited. I am a tremendous believer in the hidden potential in all of us. We all have access to our own genius which is Paul's premise in this book. The key is to be able to both realize what your genius is and to unleash it. Paul's genius is unleashed through his written word. For those who have had the privilege of knowing and working with Paul, we recognize a unique and unusual man. While his physical presence might be considered daunting to some, Paul is in fact a gentle giant. A poet, a published author, a loving husband and a giving leader in his field, Paul has captured his years of learning and growth in this marvelous book and is sharing his wisdom with all of us. Paul's background includes 25 years of leadership coaching in Fortune 500 and mid-sized companies. In his personal growth, Paul was part of a groundbreaking entrepreneurial company that established leadership practices that helped chart the life course that Paul is now on. As Paul discovered his genius, he unselfishly has shared this knowledge with hundreds of others—individuals, coaches, teams and leaders.

As I read the book, I was struck by how masterfully Paul takes us on a journey from "Comparative Thought" to "Being in the Zone" to "Integrative Presence." You'll learn how to let go of comparative thought. You'll learn to recognize your zone and when you are in it. And ultimately, you'll learn how to be in your zone all of the time as your natural state of mind in the business environment or any other environment. Integrative presence will result in significantly improved personal performance and being happier.

As a charter attendee of Paul's Unleashing Genius workshop retreat, I was struck by the notion that when we are in the moment, in our "zone," we are unleashing our genius. What is it that might prevent us from being in the zone all of the time? If we can find a way to get us there quickly, why can't we operate from that place all of the time? The realization I reached was that the only thing preventing me from being in that state all of the time is me. So now one might question "all of the time" as to how realistic it might be to be in the zone "all of the time." This is what Paul has defined as "Integrative Presence." A lofty goal one might surmise. And yet, why not? These are questions for the reader to ponder and to seek answers to; and such thought is of course on a personal level.

However, just thinking about Integrative Presence may be too limiting. Why not engage those who know you best to acknowledge you when you are in your zone? Positive reinforcement can only help to move you towards your Integrative Presence. When we are in Integrative Presence, we just go there without thinking consciously about it.

In my personal journey through a second career as a business coach, I have committed myself to serving others and helping them to reach their full potential, as has Paul. We share this common personal mission statement. Paul's book has captured the heart and soul of his 25 years of business coaching. I realized my personal genius and I am out in the world, sharing that with those who give me the opportunity to do so. You will learn a lot about yourself when you read Unleashing Genius, and you will want to read it over and over again to remind yourself that you can always be in your own personal zone—you just have to flip your own switch! Read on and discover for yourself.

Steve Heckler
Founder and President
Steve Heckler Associates
www.stevehecklerassoc.com
October, 2007

TABLE OF CONTENTS

INTRODUCTION

Creating realities in leadership
that were previously undiscovered

I have worked with leaders, mostly CEO's, on the frontlines, helping them lead through both difficult and successful times. I have advised them, coached them, taken them off-site with their teams, and helped them discover their business strategies, their genius, and ways to turn their ideas into living reality. During this journey, I have realized that leadership is one of the most difficult pursuits for which a person can commit.

The world is competitive and constantly changing. Those who choose to lead must find paths to success, and often have to lead reluctant, critical and stubborn people on missions that can be elusive. They must turn the visions that only exist in their minds into social and economic realities that enliven their companies and countries.

Transforming the Barn

My first lesson in leadership came from my father. When I was in junior high school, my grandfather and grandmother wanted to move from England to our farm to be close to my mom and dad. We needed a house for them, and also had to double the size of the main family home and build a cold storage unit for our fruits and vegetables. We had little money, but my dad discovered an old cow barn that was scheduled to be destroyed to make room for an expanding university.

150 feet long, two stories and all we needed to fulfill our dream

The university officials said we could tear down the building and take away all the lumber, which was considerable, if we gave them one thousand dollars and cleared the site by fall. I was fourteen and my brother was nine years old. My dad agreed and we began.

My dad had already noticed that this "Gentlemen's Cow Barn" was full of lumber. Two by twelve inch boards, double-wall construction, and tongue and groove carved planks on the inside walls. It was 150 feet long and 25 feet wide, with two stories and built better than most homes. It was a treasure-trove of lumber.

Like a good leader, my dad continuously explained to us the benefits of taking this barn apart, one board at a time, and using these supplies to build a home for my grandparents. He explained that not only would we do that, we would double the size of our house and, most important to us, create a family room that would contain a pool table, ping pong table, dartboard, and many other wonderful games for us and our friends. We were motivated to work all summer from sunrise to sunset and had no idea that most people would consider this an impossible task. My dad was so confident and inspiring that we did not hesitate for a moment.

We rigged a trailer with a twelve-foot hitch to make room for the long planks, loaded the suburban with tools, and started at the top of the barn and worked our way down. We saved every nail, plank and beam; my nine-year-old brother was in charge of straightening nails. We finished on time and built the house for my grandparents, extended our house, and we and our friends played in the family room for years after. Additionally, we sold used lumber for many years. I found out when I grew up that my dad had never done anything like this before.

My grandfather, me and my father in triumph towards the end

We did not have the right tools or experience, and time was impossibly short. What we did have was a compelling vision for the future, which gave us motivation and desire, and the confidence that we could do anything.

Collaborating With Nature

Helping my father make a living from farming also contributed to my understanding of leadership and business. We maintained the farm, grew our products, and sold them at the Farmer's Market. Our investments were significant, and our income depended on how well we learned to collaborate with nature.

As farmers, we were reminded constantly that you cannot fool Mother Nature. You must collaborate with her flow to succeed. Seeds planted too early will bloom and be killed by a frost. Seeds planted too late will not achieve full production. Each season has a different rhythm and starting point. You must have a certain presence to notice what is happening each year to plant your seeds at the right time, and you must work hard to nurture you're planting. It gave me a keen sense of the power of the universe that we are all part of, and how collaborating with its principles is essential for success.

There are chains of cause and effect that have their own intelligence in all aspects of life; nature for the farmer and the market place for the business person. As leaders plant seeds in business, they must observe existing reality; combine it with their intention, and work to influence the flow of their market place. At the same time, they must convince people to follow them on the mission.

We knew successful farmers who could smell the spring air and know when to plant; they always had the best crops. I have also known leaders who knew when to pull stock out of the market. It is the same set of skills, and in this book you will learn how to master these skills and integrate them into your leadership.

Discovering Realities Previously Unknown

Starting with my experiences on our farm working with my father to build a business around the flow of nature, I have experienced many of the secrets of leadership. During my work with Fortune 500 CEO's, I stimulated and experienced great accomplishments. I learned from my experience building companies, and infused the wisdom I collected into the challenges of each of my leaders. I have also studied philosophy, science, psychology and the wisdom of the ages to contribute to these understandings. But most important, in moments of what I call "Integrative Presence," insight uncovered new realities for leaders. In these moments we discovered, as Albert Einstein said, "Realities previously unknown." This wisdom is the heart of this book.

I have discovered, with the help of my mentors, that you can "Unleash Genius" in each leader and organization that is both natural and hard to find. It is genius that once discovered seems obvious, but prior to discovery, is invisible. It is genius which unleashes unimaginable levels of performance that flows like a dancer who has reached mastery. It is often covered, and takes discipline to find, yet it is graceful and easy once achieved.

Genius is, as I define it, collaboration with the natural flow that extends from the present, and from the knowledge, intention and consciousness of an individual or group. It is achieved through Integrative Presence, which allows you to integrate all the realities of the moment simultaneously while combining them with your intention. Those who master this will Unleash Genius within themselves, the people who follow them, and their team, to create new realities once unimaginable.

In this book I share what I have learned about discovering and manifesting genius. I hope you find these chapters provocative and useful. But please don't accept or reject what I say; use these thoughts to stimulate your own discovery. Think along with me so we can discover new and even greater realities. Explore the unknown within yourself, with the intention of creating original thoughts that come from connecting to the deep wisdom and genius within you.

To help you on this quest, I give you an ancient Taoist riddle that was often given to monks as part of their study about life. It contains a basic truth about how life works, which is the key understanding for leaders.

"First there is a mountain, then there is no mountain, and then there is."

The elements of this lesson are woven throughout this book. See if you can find them as you read and reflect.

Let go of what you know as you read and capture new thoughts in a journal. Share these thoughts with your friends and join the explorative dialogue on our website and in my Leadership Institute. One insight creates another even greater and, with discipline, the collective wisdom grows. I invite you to join us in discovering and creating new realities that will create understandings about leadership that were previously undiscovered.

www.pauldavidwalker.com

CREATING
NEW REALITIES

One of the purposes of life
is to extend the universe with beauty.

Just as Camelot rose out of the darkness in mythology to create a shining kingdom on a hill, real creations have risen all around the world. Their monuments, like the myth of the Lady of The Lake holding Excalibur for the next true King in the depths of the still water, remind us of great possibilities that wait to be created. They stand as evidence of what has been and could be again.

England's great Cathedrals spread out across the green land, built as monuments to a great idea, are now surrounded by cities and often passed unnoticed by locals. Though their greatness has faded, what was built between 1066 and 1400 in a flurry of passion stands as an awesome reminder of what great leadership can create.

One can only imagine the inspiration and fervor that lead people to create these beautiful places of worship all across Great Britain. Christianity arrived from France with a burst of creativity that not only created Cathedrals, but the Free Masons who built them.

A New Way

It all started when the Emperor of Rome watched as Christians refused to fight in the arena. They turned the other cheek and died before they would kill. These followers told stories of the Prince of Peace in a time of vengeance and sport killing. They carried the words of their leader, Jesus of Nazareth, who said at the moment of his death, "Forgive them for they know not what they do." This new idea of love and forgiveness converted the Emperor of the greatest empire of all time to Christianity.

From the seat of Rome to the plains of Salisbury, the inspiration of this new idea in a time of darkness rang out like a clear bell, and created expressions of beauty and devotion whose towers still ring out across the world today. An idea that rises from deep wisdom manifests first in the hearts of people, then in their actions and creations. You can see it all around the world.

Rome itself rose from the idea of creating a republic ruled, not by an Emperor, but by the Senate. It was governed by the nobles from each region around the world who would join together to create a republic modeled after Greece. Rome was not a city; it was an idea whose manifestations are still evident, spanning Christianity and Western Civilization as we know it today.

Renaissance

As Europe was climbing out of the dark ages between the 15th and 16th Centuries, first in Italy, then in France, England and other rising nations, the Renaissance swept across Europe and changed the course of civilization. A rebirth of art and science began as Marco Polo brought back tales and riches from the Far East. Silks, science and spices flowed into Italy. Ideas from classical civilizations were combined with new science. Leonardo De Vinci designed a flying machine, created great art and science, and became the first "Universal Man" who mastered many disciplines.

Great sculptures, art and science spread across Europe, but not without resistance. Science seemed heretical because for the first time wisdom seemed to be separate from God's inspiration. Yet most of those early scientists did not deny the grace that comes from God; they wanted to begin to understand exactly how the universe worked. Instruments and the scientific method began to extend human knowledge. This was the dawn of science and lead to the Industrial Revolution, which became centered in England.

Fight for Freedom

As reflected in the mythology of Camelot, the people of the British Isles longed for freedom. They held back the Romans from final victory behind Hadrian's Wall. The Celts held back waves of invaders and still have a strong spirit in Cornwall, Wales, Scotland and Ireland. The world can still hear William Wallace cry out the word, "freedom," which defines the spirit of the people who live in these isles.

In 1805 England's freedom was again threatened by Napoleon, who had gathered 90,000 troops on the coast of France waiting for naval protection. Fortunately for England, the ships would not come because Lord Horatio Nelson pursued the combined French and Spanish fleet at Cape Trafalgar in one of the largest naval battles in history. Nelson felt that England's very survival was at stake when his ship sailed directly into Napoleon's conscripted fleet, which outnumbered his. The signal flags spelled out, "England expects that every man will do his duty" and the sailors cheered. Nelson led the battle personally by riding his ship, Victory, ahead of all the other ships into the French line.

The French fleet failed, in part, because the English were better trained on the canons; but mostly because the English believed in what they were giving their lives to uphold: Freedom vs. Tyranny. As a result of this victory, English became a global language and England's ships ruled the oceans. England established an empire larger than any on Earth before or since. The Empire was based on the ideals of freedom, dignity and the rule of law.

While Nelson was defending England, a colony of Englishmen had won their freedom based on another new idea that took freedom to a new level; "All men are created equal and have the right to life, liberty and the pursuit of happiness." Rule by a government "by the people and for the people" was a unique and revolutionary idea that seemed like foolishness to the monarchies of Europe; but it released a wave of creativity and inventiveness that is unparalleled in history.

The idea of freedom to pursue your dreams and be free from tyranny of all kinds attracted millions of people from all around the world. They built a nation that is the most creative, innovative and economically productive in history. The idea of freedom has spread throughout the world, and is at the heart of a global revolution.

Twilight Club

In 1870 the "Twilight Club" was founded by Herbert Spencer and Ralph Waldo Emerson and was active until 1921, when it was renamed "Society of Arts and Science," and reorganized by Walter Russell, Edwin Markham and Thomas J. Watson (Founder of IBM). It continued to stimulate leaders until 1935 when it lost momentum.

Noted members of this organization who participated in global discourse were: Walt Whitman, Edwin Markham, Andrew Carnegie, Mark Twain, Walter Russell, James Howard Bridge, John Dewey, Robert Collier, Cornelius Vanderbilt, Theodore Roosevelt, Calvin Coolidge, and many other thinkers and leaders who formed the foundations for modern civilization which we live in today.

These thought leaders created such organizations and movements as: Boy Scouts in England and America, Rotary, Kiwanis, the Lions Clubs, Better Business Bureaus, sweat shop elimination, advertising censorship (honesty), child welfare, and IBM's THINK campaign. They moved the leaders of business and politics towards higher ethics and morality, creating higher levels of thinking that drove the freedom and creativity which lead to our thriving global economy.

We hope to create this kind of impact with those who read this book, dialogue on our website and join us in our Leadership Institute.

Great Ideas Create Great Realities

The collective wisdom of these thought leaders set the stage for the liberty and creativity we experience today. Who would have imagined during the Renaissance that, at a touch of a button on a cell phone from California, you could be talking to a friend on his way to the Taj Mahal in India and he would sound like he was next door? Movies, TV shows, and volumes of music are downloaded onto a tiny iPod created by the people of Apple, Steve Jobs' monument to creativity.

Great ideas have created history. The Israelites sought freedom from Egypt. The Buddha found freedom from suffering. Rome established "The Republic." Zheng He, commander of the Ming Armada in 1402, sought to establish virtue and free trade. The scientists from the Renaissance, and those who followed their ideas, still seek a true understanding of how the universe works.

All these civilizations, and many others unmentioned, have risen upon great ideas. Insight came in a mountain cave for Mohammed; revelations from 40 days and nights in the desert inspired Jesus; the awakening of Buddha, while sitting under a tree, turned into thought and created a great civilization. Many insights unknown to us stimulated thoughts that inspired actions that created all the buildings, art and beauty on this Earth. These ideas, taken to heart, stimulated men and women to act in extraordinary ways, creating victories, products, peace of mind, companies and civilizations. We will explore together in this book the source of great ideas and how to manifest those ideas into living reality.

Nothing Can Stay

As Robert Frost says in his poem, "Nothing Gold Can Stay," most empires fall. Nothing seems to last forever.

Nature's first green is gold
Her hardest hue to hold,
But only so an hour.
So leaf subsides to leaf
So Eden sank to grief
Nothing gold can stay.

What causes the fall? The young Arthur in his anger and pride broke Excalibur, the unbreakable sword of truth. The dream of Rome faded and the city itself was plundered. Was it another great idea, or the lack of connection to the original, that destroyed Rome and other civilizations?

As a leader, one should know how to create great ideas that inspire people to create and how to prevent or delay the fall. You may not be building an empire or a great religion, but to succeed, you must create a desire in the hearts of people to create something. Your desired creation may be your life, a happy family, a new product, a company, or a new civilization. You must learn the secrets of creating and manifesting before you can give it birth. You must know how to evoke the sword of truth from the deep stillness of the mythological lake that is within your soul.

Unleash Your Genius

This book is designed to help you unleash the kind of genius that sparked much of human history. Its purpose is to find the true calling within you, so that you may lead others on great quests that release their genius to create and extend this world with beauty.

Don't put it down because you are only an ordinary person, because all the great leaders in history were once ordinary. Nelson was not born a Lord; he was knighted for his great deeds. The founders of the United States were simple men who put their lives and fortunes on the line for ideas that changed the course of history.

I am an ordinary man who, with the help of committed mentors, coaches, and personal reflection, came from a Lock House in the dust of industrial England to counsel the CEO's of Fortune 500 companies. If you use the journal that goes with this book for your own reflection, discuss these ideas with your friends and family, and practice what you learn with rigor, you will unleash the genius that I assure you everyone has. You may find yourself on quests that change the course of your life, family, company or history. The choice is yours.

Imagine a world where most people have unleashed their genius and are passionately creating their dreams in synergy with each other. What could we achieve? How would our world be different for our children and grandchildren? Certainly only a few during the Dark Ages could imagine what the Renaissance began. Most could not have imagined air flight, but De Vinci did. Who would have envisioned cell phones, thousands of towering cities full of creativity, and the level of freedom we now enjoy. Century after century people sit quietly seeking insight, receive it, and create the future. One reality is sure:

> *You cannot solve a problem at the same level of awareness that created it.*
> —*Albert Einstein*

This has been proven over history. Imagine how different the world would be if we were to reach a tipping point with most people having unleashed their genius. We could speculate on what our world would be, but for now let us begin with you.

At the end of each chapter I ask you to reflect on what was said, journal your thoughts and have discussions with friends and family. I don't want you to believe the things I say, I want you to use them to stimulate your thinking to help you create a roadmap into your own unique genius. If you were training for an Olympic event, your coach would tell you that there is no substitute for practice. I am telling you the same thing. You must stop and reflect, connect with something beyond yourself, journal your thoughts, and dialogue with others.

After you have spent time journaling your insights, or at anytime while reading the book, go to your journal and create action steps and practices you feel will help you integrate your positive insights into your life. Don't feel you have to develop a practice for each insight, or be in a rush to add practices. Wait until something occurs to you, and if necessary, come back to the appropriate chapter and create practices. Please use your journal, to deepen your insights and integrate them into your life. There is no substitute for practice.

If nothing occurs to you, don't try to force something, just continue reading. As insights, practices and action steps occur, record them in your journal. If you prefer, read the entire book and then come back to your journal and build practices. Please share your insights and practices with us on the Leadership Forum in our Institute website at www.pauldavidwalker.com.

To create new realities a leader must:
- Have a compelling purpose and mission
- A clear vision of the benefits of that purpose
- The ability to communicate the benefits to the team at all levels
- Confidence combined with humility
- Be open to new ways of creating the mission

CONNECTING
WITH WISDOM

"There is one mind common to all individual men. Every man is an inlet to the same and to all of the same. Who hath access to this universal mind is a party to all that is or can be done, for this is the only and sovereign agent."
—*Ralph Waldo Emerson*

As discussed in the previous chapter, it is clear that extraordinary ideas create great civilizations and accomplishments. We will explore together in this book the source of these ideas, and the state-of-mind that unleashes genius and leads to the great accomplishments of leaders throughout time.

After watching Florence Joyner win the hundred meter dash, the TV interviewer showed a super-slow-motion playback of her run. She was about equal with the field through the middle of the run, and then she leaped out way ahead of the field to win the race. The interviewer played the run again, and just as she put distance between her and the field, the interviewer stopped the tape and pointed to the screen and asked, "What happens right here?" Florence answered, "I just let go, and go with the flow."

After the start-up of the race, she slipped into what sports coaches call "The Zone" and, of course, her performance accelerated dramatically. Sports coaches try to teach athletes to achieve this state. Being able to find your way into "The Zone" is critical for success as an athlete. Some respond to pressure by "clutching," and thereby reduce performance, and others slip into "The Zone." Michael Jordan was famous for performing better under pressure, as are many successful athletes. When a shot was needed to win the game, he would say, "Give me the ball."

Integrative Presence

Sports coaches realize that if athletes have to think in a comparative manner, they will be moving too slowly, or worse, frightening themselves with their thinking like, "I have got to make this shot." This kind of thinking, which can be called Comparative Thought, is just not fast enough. They train their clients to get into "The Zone," which in business I call **"Integrative Presence."**

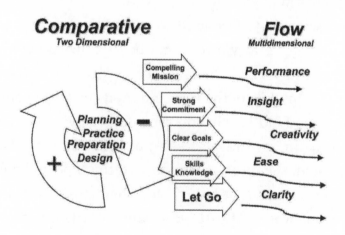

The key is knowing when and how to let go of comparative thought. As illustrated above, there are a number of common keys to letting go of comparative thought and moving into **Integrative Presence.** Some of those are:

- Commitment to an important mission
- Clear goals that the person believes are important to achieve
- The stress of a situation that forces action
- Danger that must be responded to
- Being out in nature for long periods of time
- Meditating and yoga techniques

The truth is anything can cause your conscious mind to let go of comparative thought. It would be impossible to catalogue all experiences people have had. What is important is to know the difference between the two states of mind and practicing so that you can operate more often in **Integrative Presence.**

When I have asked people to describe how they feel when they experience Integrative Presence, they say things like: confident, at peace, exhilarated, powerful, graceful, and present. Some report a slow motion effect as time slows. Kareem Abdul-Jabbar told how the five seconds he had to win the NBA championship with one shot seemed like five minutes. He felt relaxed, as if he had all the time in the world, yet he appeared to move like lightning to the rest of the world—the very definition of Integrative

Presence. His creativity, within these few precious seconds, was nothing less than pure genius. He was integrating the skills he had learned over the years, his desire to make the shot, and the flow of the moment.

This state of mind seems to be the natural state for humans. The art of getting into this state of mind is letting go of comparative thought. As you let go, this state of mind just takes over. You don't need to train yourself to experience Integrative Presence, you merely need to "let go" as Florence Joyner said. This state just seems to take over your consciousness and supercharges your performance because of its integrative nature.

Sports create highly charged environments. They are designed to bring out the best in people. But can this state be achieved outside this arena? Certainly, if these states of mind that seem to create super human results can be created in one area of life, they should be able to be created in others. While the environment is particularly right for this kind of performance in sports, it is not beyond or separate from this "real world" we all operate within.

Knowing the Difference

When I was working as a leadership consultant to Don Ross, Chairman and CEO of New York Life, during the summer of 1987, many people were coming to me questioning the Chairman's actions. He had asked the investment department to slowly move all investments out of the stock market into conservative investments. This frustrated his investment team because the stock market was at an all time high and their competitors were using "High Yield Bonds" and stocks to create gains much greater than New York Life's. They wanted to play in the game, and Don Ross was telling them to step back.

Many came to me, as Don's coach, to suggest I persuade him of the foolishness of his actions. I explained that I was his leadership coach and had little knowledge of the financial markets, but encouraged them to speak directly to Don. However, no matter how people pleaded, he would not change course. Several key players resigned and went to more "progressive" companies.

On October 7, 1987, while I was on site at New York Life, the market crashed. It was the biggest crash since the Great Depression. But New York Life had moved most of its investments out of the stock market and had not invested in any "High Yield Bonds," known later as "Junk Bonds." Don Ross was now considered a genius. The financial gain was enormous.

A week or so later, I asked Don how he knew to pull all of the company's investments out of the stock market three months before the October 1987 crash. He said, "I just knew it couldn't last." Everyone in his world thought he was wrong, yet he had the wisdom and courage to do what he felt was right.

He later went on to explain that, as Chairman and CEO, he was continuously bombarded with "experts" trying to convince him of completely different strategic directions.

Each had incredible credentials and a good story, yet each recommended different directions. The only tool he had to make the final decision was his instinct, or intuition. He said, "Whenever I have gone against my intuition, I have regretted it." Don certainly would have agreed with Buddha when he said,

"Believe nothing, no matter where you read it or who said it, even if I said it, unless it agrees with your reason and your own common sense."

Don Ross explained to me, "The key to wisdom is to know the difference between your wild hopes and fears and common sense, intuition or true wisdom." They often seem the same, but they are not. There is a distinct difference in the feeling. One comes from the Ego and insecurity, and the other comes from Wisdom. Great leaders learn the difference and develop the courage to act. Don had found ways to live in Integrative Presence, or at least he was able to find that state of mind when he needed insight. When I met with him over the years, he was often in the state of Integrative Presence. He was warm, yet seemed to be able to see through people. Insightful, yet he moved with grace and ease.

All the great leaders I have worked with know how to achieve the state of Integrative Presence, even though they may not understand the nature of this state of mind. They know that they must be connected to something that supercharges their own knowledge. They speak reverently about this connection in private, but rarely talk about it to the press. It just seems too outside the norm for stockholders and the public. But knowing and connecting to wisdom through Integrative Presence is essential for leaders in business today. Markets move quickly, often with little warning, and the wise leader is two or three moves ahead of the competition, prepared to take advantage of trends that are emerging.

In New York Life's case, the gains were in the billions. Those gains were entirely dependent on Don Ross knowing the difference between his ego, fears and true wisdom. There are a hundred stories like this. I am sure you have heard the phrases like: "gut feel," "gut check," "trusting my instincts," and "going with what I know to be true."

A Natural State of Mind

Connecting with wisdom is both mysterious and highly effective in business. Making this connection comes naturally when a leader can move from comparative thought to Integrative Presence. It enables you to make decisions quickly that drive extraordinary outcomes. The difference between being in "The Zone" and "Integrative Presence" is that Integrative Presence extends over a longer period of time, and can become a natural part of a leader's state of mind in the business environment or any other.

The Associated Press reported the following story:
Saturday, January 1, 2005 Posted: 6:25 PM EST (2325 GMT)

BANGKOK, Thailand (AP)—Knowledge of the ocean and its currents passed down from generation to generation of a group of Thai fishermen known as the Morgan sea gypsies saved an entire village from the Asian tsunami, a newspaper said Saturday.

By the time killer waves crashed over southern Thailand last Sunday the entire 181 population of their fishing village had fled to a temple in the mountains of South Surin Island, English language Thai daily The Nation reported.

"The elders told us that if the water recedes fast it will reappear in the same quantity in which it disappeared," 65-year-old village chief Sarmao Kathalay told the paper.

So while in some places along the southern coast, Thais headed to the beach when the sea drained out of beaches— the first sign of the impending tsunami—to pick up fish left flapping on the sand, the gypsies headed for the hills.

Few people in Thailand have a closer relationship with the sea than the Morgan sea gypsies, who spend each monsoon season on their boats plying the waters of the Andaman Sea from India to Indonesia and back to Thailand.

Between April and December, they live in shelters on the shore surviving by catching shrimp and spear fishing. At boat launching festivals each May, they ask the sea for forgiveness.

The emergency rescue teams who first responded to the disaster areas were astonished by the lack of dead animals among the human casualties. The general accepted reason for this, by wildlife experts, is that the animals sensed the pending doom and fled to higher ground. The amazing thing is that the animals sensed the disaster so early that they did not need to scamper to safety in such a hurried pace as to draw attention to themselves. Copyright 2005 The Associated Press.

Both in the case of Don Ross and the Morgan sea gypsies, there seems to be a combination of connection to some understanding or flow, beyond what we would call normal and the existing knowledge of the person. Don Ross came up through the Investment Department, and the gypsies listened to their elders and were connected to the sea for generations. Even in Florence Joyner's case, she could not have won by being in "The Zone" alone, without her training and understanding of sprinting.

If I was playing basketball with Michael Jordan and he was clutching, worrying, in terrible mental health, unable to achieve a state of Integrative Presence, while I was totally there, who would win? Clearly, Michael Jordan would win because his training and knowledge of the game is so superior to mine. But if he were playing someone who was his equal, the lack of connection to this state of mind would surely end in his defeat.

It is reported that the perceptual field of athletes in this state of mind widens considerably. They can sense their position on the court. It almost seems like they have eyes in the back of their heads. Leaders who can will themselves into Integrative Presence seem to be able to see through people.

Connection without Thought

When humans are involved in this state of mind, it seems there is always a combination of knowledge and intuition. However, it seems the animals that survived the tsunami sensed the pending doom without language to pass on information. Yet their connection to nature told them to flee well in advance of the approach of the killer waves. Therefore, there must be a force that carries some form of information that can be perceived without knowledge. Don Ross was one of the very few who could sense the coming market crash. Others certainly had as much, if not more, knowledge of the financial markets than he. Yet they did not sense the pending financial doom.

There are geniuses throughout history who seemed to have abilities way beyond the knowledge they possessed. There are child prodigies who just start playing the piano, and normal people who just seem to know things without formal education or training. What is going on here? It is important to understand this mysterious process, if you are going to unleash your genius or the genius of others.

Three Elements

The following model is an attempt to make distinctions that will help us to understand the elements that lead to genius. This simple model summarizes much of the philosophical and psychological thought of our time. As you read this, try to reflect on times in your life when each of these elements was present.

There are three basic elements that form our perceived realities.

The Life Force: Emerson called it **"The Great Intelligence,"** which is my personal favorite. Some call it "Universal Mind;" others refer to it as a God-given grace or intelligence. It is the driving force behind life itself, an energy that enlivens all things and is available to all.

Scientists are now able to measure it and see its effects on life, but still do not know from where it comes or exactly how it works. However, it is clearly at work in all human endeavors. We will not go into its source or origin in this book, but since it is a reality of how the Universe works, we must consider this force in our discussions. It seems to be the extra ingredient that we connect with when we achieve Integrative Presence or have understandings that are beyond our knowledge base.

Consciousness: Our ability to perceive the world through our senses and mind. It is what brings the world around us to light. Without it we would still exist, but would not be aware of our existence or the existence of other things.

Thought: Gives us the ability to understand what we perceive. With thought, we make distinctions between that which we perceive. Without thought, much of what we are conscious of would blur together in a formless mass. With distinctions made by thought, we organize that which we are conscious of, and create our psychological, social and physical realities. Plants have the life force and consciousness, but not thought as we know it. They cannot make comparisons, nor are they able to create.

The way we mix these three elements determines our state of mind, which has a significant influence on our perceived reality. This is important for a leader to understand because one of the keys to success is creating a team which is committed to something larger than itself. If people are creating their own realities that do not support the mission of a business or organization, then it will be difficult to move hundreds, if not thousands, of people in the same direction, and even more difficult to expand their consciousness.

The following graphic illustrates:

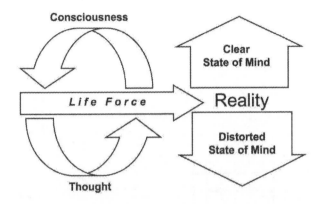

When our consciousness is focused on or obsessed with thoughts, and is not well-mixed with the "Great Intelligence," our reality is not complete and is distorted. Thoughts, and the knowledge that comes from thought, or a matrix of beliefs and assumptions that come from thought, is not enough. This "Great Intelligence" must be included.

Thought Reduces Consciousness

When leaders are not using Integrative Presence, the source of their thought tends to be their thinking, or belief systems that come from their thinking, as illustrated in the following graphic. Thought hardens into a grid of beliefs and assumptions that no longer represent reality.

Thought by its nature reduces consciousness. It cannot express the full measure of reality. If your new thoughts are only sourced from your old thoughts and beliefs, then the level of distortion increases. Most people circle between the grid formed by their thought and a distorted reality. They form a grid of beliefs and assumptions, and distort reality to conform.

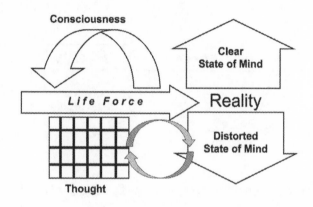

Leaders cannot afford to have distorted realities. They must become masters of **Integrative Presence,** which integrates the **Great Intelligence.** Consciousness then uses thought to express the insight or understanding that comes from this state of mind vs. using thought as the base of understanding. Thoughts can create or point to possible new realities, but they are not reality itself. Most make the mistake of believing in their own thoughts or the thoughts of others. A wise Buddhist said, when referring to Buddhism, "Buddhism is like the raft to get to the other side of the river. It is not the other side of the river." Likewise, business strategies and plans are the raft, not the other side of the river. Many mistake their ideas for reality, and lose sight of reality; like those who lingered on the beach after the ocean pulled way back.

Thought Can Block Common Sense

When the animals and the Morgan sea gypsies were heading for high ground, most were only driven by an intuitive knowledge which did not include the intellectual possibility of a tsunami. In the case of the animals, the absence of comparative thought gave them a clear channel to the impending disaster. No thoughts or beliefs interfered with the wisdom we might call instinct. The Morgan sea gypsies, like the animals, are less attached to their thoughts, and were able to act with the wisdom that the tourists and others had lost touch with.

Tourists and others were not able to sense the oncoming wave of destruction, even though there were very clear signals flowing along the currents of the life force. The Great Intelligence was speaking, but most could not hear. They were locked into whatever routine or desires dominated their consciousness. Most were completely caught up in their thoughts and only began to flee when the wall of water appeared.

In 1987, most everyone was exuberant with the growth of the financial markets. The elements of the crash were in place and visible to Don Ross, but not to most. Most were distracted with their own success and the glory of the "Go-Go 80's." When consciousness focuses only on thoughts that often circle on themselves, much is missed. Not taking into account the vast knowledge available in this mysterious intelligence can lead to disaster and unhappiness.

The problem is that this "Perceived Reality" created by our thoughts does not appear to be "perceived" to most. It is the only reality they know, and is seen as actual reality instead of a cognitive distortion. As Don Ross said, "We need to know the difference between self-created realities and "the reality."

Since people always want to be "right" and see, feel or hear their own conceived reality, and do not realize it is only a conception, they find it hard to see other greater realities, like shifts in the market place creating opportunity. They become locked into a false reality constructed by only their limited knowledge and need to be right.

A leader of an organization, who is trying to create realities that will drive the success of their business, cannot afford this limited view of life. That leader must become connected in every way to the market and the force that flows through that market, just like the force that warned the animals to flee to high ground before the tsunami.

Additionally, a leader would be wise to become a master of expanding peoples' consciousness as it relates to their business. Vast changes in the market place are constantly occurring and leaders need all the help they can get. Having teams of leaders who are able to sense changes early will magnify the chances of success. Maintaining a balance between the life force, consciousness, and thought is the key to success in all aspects of life, but is especially powerful when teams of people develop this kind of awareness.

Creating an organization full of high-performance teams of people solving tactical problems with this level of awareness, while the leadership focuses on strategy, is a powerful combination. As the leadership sees the future path by its connection to the flow of the market place, the management team and employees see the short-term moves that will lead to successful implementation. These kinds of corporate teams work powerfully, like a championship sports team. They can move quickly responding to shifting business needs that are created to account for shifts in the market place. This is a truly high-performance business team.

Illustrated in the following graphic are the three principles mentioned above in a 4 by 4 matrix. The life force is expressed as an ever-expanding constant. Consciousness and thought are variables. It takes a high level of consciousness, which brings a line of sight to more of reality, and strong thought, which enables distinctions within the field of consciousness that can position the company, team or individual for success.

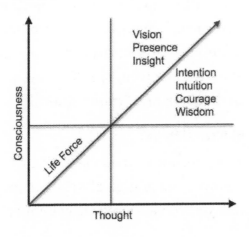

For example, a leader with a strong thought process, who is not conscious of the company's position in a changing market place, can create and articulate a vision that does not position the company correctly. Teams who follow this articulate vision will follow the unconscious leader off the cliff.

A highly conscious leader who cannot use thought to articulate his vision of the market opportunity is also ineffective. The lack of clear expression of the mission and vision the leader sees will cause the team to be scattered and out of focus, trying to follow, but without a compass.

What is Genius?

The title of this book is "Unleashing Genius." Genius is something that is available to everyone. It is the combination of high levels of consciousness combined with the "Life Force" or as Emerson says, "The Great Intelligence," which creates profound thoughts and a clear line of sight to reality. The entry point to unleashing genius is "Integrative Presence." Thoughts that are not driven by a deep consciousness of this intelligence are not effective, and often feed on themselves, blinding one to true reality and leading to disaster and unhappiness.

How Do You Unleash Genius?

While there is no formula, it is clear from the preceding that it has to do with letting go of attachment to thoughts and beliefs that you have stored in your memory. When I was working with a fashion design company, the CEO explained to me that, though the Chief Operating Officer was very effective at his work, he had alienated the rest of the team. He often falsely accused people of sabotaging his operation and other similar things. His job was on the line, and the CEO asked me if I could work with him.

When I first met him, he was on his best behavior, and I could see this was a sweet and loving man. I asked him about his family, and he described each in a loving manner with a twinkle in his eyes. I continued to ask questions that built rapport between us and, as he shared one lovely story, I would ask questions that would lead to another. As I listened to him, he seemed to light up. I could clearly see his inner genius and told him how his stories touched me. He was so natural and flowing in the way he dealt with his family in the moments he described to me. It was clear that he was a sweet, loving man whose love and kindness was his genius.

Then I started asking him questions about his teammates and his state of mind darkened. His paranoia began to intensify as he explained how people were trying to get him. It was hard to see the loving, easy-going man that I had first seen. His stories seemed to make sense so I listened and took notes, but I never lost sight of the warm, loving man I had seen as he described his family. In working with the rest of the team, I found that many of his stories about them were unfounded, or highly exaggerated. One of his teammates said to me, "Did you know his entire family was killed during the holocaust in death camps?"

The next time I met with him, I asked him about his experience during World War II. He explained that he was the only survivor, and that in order to survive, he had to escape, and in the process, had to kill two guards. He was only 14 years old. He went on to tell me a little about his mother and father and a few other family members who were murdered in the gas chambers. I could hardly hold back my tears, and in sharing this moment, our connection deepened.

He went on to explain that he had met a Russian soldier as he made his way east. That soldier had saved his life by putting him on the Trans Siberian Railroad, which eventually led to a refugee camp in China. He spent five years in this camp and found his way to New York City. He worked hard, and climbed to the top of one of the best fashion design and production companies in the city. Now he was concerned that he might lose his job.

It became clear to me that the suspicion he held for his peers was connected to his terrible life experiences. I told him that it was a miracle that he had succeeded, and that given his life experience, I understood how he might have a low level of trust for others.

Over time, I helped him see that he was no longer in danger, and that the feelings he still held onto from his past were influencing his behavior in the present. I can't remember exactly what I said to him, but suddenly he understood. He saw how his attachment to his thoughts and beliefs from the past was distorting his present reality.

As insight came to him, I carefully explained how the CEO and his peers valued him. The only problem was his lack of trust for them which he displayed with his anger. If he could only let go of this and understand that he was safe here and now, he would be a success. I then shared how I could see the loving spirit within him, and we both had a moment.

His anger gradually went away, and his loving spirit often showed on his face. Because of the way he connected with people, his business activities became two or three times more effective. People trusted him, and the loving spirit he displayed allowed full engagement of his skills in the industry. The darkness lifted, and everyone wanted to play the game of business with him.

About a month later, as I was working with someone else, his assistant came in and said that his wife was in the conference room and she wanted to talk to me. I was concerned, but when I met with her, she thanked me for bringing her husband back to her. She said that his loving spirit was what she fell in love with, and it had been hidden over the last few years. She hugged me and left me in the conference room. I realized in that moment that my connection with his loving spirit, which is his genius, was what allowed him to let go of the beliefs from the past.

Since then, I have learned that all people have some special genius that is often covered, and that seeing through the mask created by their thoughts from the past and connecting with their genius is key to helping people let go. Even more important, just as Florence Joyner slips into "The Zone" naturally after she lets go, as all people let go of whatever is holding back their genius, the genius appears naturally. It is the default setting.

The grid of thoughts that held back this man's natural ability to express love and kindness was dramatic, and it seems amazing that he could let go. However, more problematic are those whose thoughts are "normal." Attachment to any grid of thoughts from the past blinds us to the present. It is more difficult to let go of what seem like positive thoughts. Thoughts that a person feels are righteous and true are blinding and harder to let go of.

Later, this man used his wealth to find that Russian soldier and brought him to New York City with much gratitude and fanfare. He was very successful, and for years my wife received beautiful dresses with special notes from this great man. Genius waits behind both "positive and negative" cognitive frameworks.

Each chapter in this book will help leaders expand their consciousness to include "The Great Intelligence" so that your thoughts and realities are clear and create expansion for you, the people around you, and the business you are committed to create.

To connect to wisdom, it is key to:

- Know the difference between your ego and wisdom
- Know the difference between your fear and wisdom
- Find and learn your personal roadmap to your wisdom
- Have the courage to act on your wisdom
- Know that the gate to wisdom is in the present moment
- Practice "Integrative Presence"

MASTERY OF THOUGHT

You Cannot Create What
You Cannot Conceive

It is clear that human thought is one of the sources of creation. Some say that thought, itself, has the power to create reality. There is plenty of evidence to support this view. All architecture, businesses, governments, art and civilizations are the product of thought. Many social scientists, psychologists and philosophers say that thought creates our reality. We cannot perceive the world around us but through our thought systems. Thought systems clearly create individual and collective realities.

Not only do thoughts create beautiful realities, they also create false and horrible realities. For example, anorexic people will look in the mirror and see fat, even though there is none. They may be starving themselves to death, but their thoughts tell them they need to lose weight in order to be accepted. This is called a cognitive distortion. Of course, this is an extreme example. But since thought drives behavior, many similar tragedies can occur.

My Genius Unleashed

A high school friend of mine in Michigan helped me realize my genius. I grew up on a farm and was not doing very well in school, while he was recognized as a genius. He could play songs from the radio on the piano by ear. He would hear something and just play it. He was recognized in many ways as the smartest kid in the class. Somehow we became best friends, and one day he came to me with a book that he decided I just had to read.

I had not read many books and wasn't that interested, but he insisted, and told me to go into his room and not come out until I had finished. It was a short book, so I complied. I was quite taken with the book, and when he asked me what I thought it meant, I explained. He asked me a lot of questions and I could see he approved of my answers. Then he stopped and said, "Paul, do you realize who this author is?" I said that I had never heard of him.

He went on to tell me that this was Albert Camus, one of the leading thinkers in western philosophy. He pointed out that I understood the meanings in this book at a deeper level than him. He said to me, "Paul, your understanding of this book is genius." That conversation changed the course of my life. I started writing poetry, went to college and created the university arts and literature magazine. He saw my genius and reflected it back to me; and his words unleashed my genius.

I went on to become a business leader, using my understanding to become a change agent and leadership consultant and coach. He went to Hollywood to pursue a career in acting. I found out many years later his career did not do well. I could not understand because he was so talented in high school and college.

A Belief Blocked His Genius

I heard stories from his wife about why he wasn't successful, but what really stopped me in my tracks was a phrase I heard many times at his 40th birthday party. Most of his friends were unsuccessful actors and the phrase I heard from many of them was, **"Truly talented people do not make it in Hollywood."** My friend had created a belief that was destroying his life, and no matter how hard I tried, I could not convince him of the folly of this belief.

Thought is the Greatest Gift and Curse

Thought can create great works of art, successful corporations and beautiful cities, but it can also block the expression of genius. It should come with a warning label.

In 1987, everyone thought the boom in the stock market would last. It did not, and many companies lost a lot of real money. Recently, people thought the Internet created a new economic paradigm that would totally change global economics. The people at Jones Town thought drinking Cool-Aid would lead to bliss. A paranoid schizophrenic sees people and hears voices that do not exist. Some countries have thought entire races of people were inferior and sought to cleanse the world of these people.

Thought creates worry, hatred and many miscalculations, as well as great success. Many companies have thought their strategy was right even in the face of declining numbers and failure. Therefore, it is worth spending the time to truly understand how thought affects our reality.

Turning Thoughts into Reality

Thought precedes action and manifestation. We need to understand how thought works because it's a key building block of enterprise. This is not the "power of positive thinking" nor is it some "new age" revelation. Our thoughts **can** become great ideas.

Sometimes, these thoughts seem to appear, as "AHAs" in what seems like a flash; others build over time. A company, a product, a way to dominate a market, a motion picture, and even a country, were once just a series of thoughts organized into a vision for the future.

We've all heard about the great success of sports teams who operate in "The Zone." To understand the thought process behind high-performing teams, we need to understand the difference between "comparative thought" and "Integrative Presence." Both are valuable in any human endeavor. Problems arise when we use them inappropriately.

Comparative Thought

When we refer to comparative thought, we mean the entire process of thinking and framing the world based upon language. This includes positive thinking, negative thinking, worry, visioning, planning and all other forms of comparison. Examples are good compared to bad, day as opposed to night. In this way, winning and losing seem inseparable in our society.

Comparative thought is the foundation for our civilization. Our ability to think in this manner has advanced the human race to great heights of achievement; without it we might still be living in caves. The difficulty comes when we confuse thought and the product of thought with living. Comparative thought is a marvelous tool, but not life itself.

What are the differences between life itself and our thoughts about life? Let's say someone with excellent writing skills describes a special experience, such as going for a swim in the warm waters of the Caribbean with a lover at their side, capturing the glances and touches of love during that evening on the beach beside a fire. How close to the reality of this experience would the writing be? Would it be anything like that sunset perience. The experience itself is "beyond words" or "beyond comparison." Thoughts about life are like a person's shadow, as opposed to the person. Our thoughts are, at best, the "shadow of life." "Life", as opposed to the "shadow of life," is found closer to the moment of experience.

From moment to moment we are living life itself, our thoughts about life, or some combination of both. When we achieve Integrative Presence, we are living closer to life itself. Our perceptions are not cluttered with comparative thoughts. We experience life with less distortion and, thereby, experience higher levels of performance.

Comparative Thought in Business

Please note that Integrative Presence is not about "positive thinking." What's wrong with a positive thinker? Nothing is wrong, as long as positive thinking doesn't turn you into a dreamer who lives in a fantasy. Dreamers have plans that rarely work out. Often when they fail, instead of learning, they just come up with another idea. The world they create in their mind is many steps from reality. That's why they seem "lightweight." They are living the shadow of life.

On the other hand, a leader who's a "negative thinker" is caught up in thoughts that create stress, frustration or anger. Decisions are influenced by these emotions and may not be in the best interest of the business. A strongly held belief about a certain strategic direction might prevent insight into an even more effective direction. When a strongly held belief becomes a conviction, we are no longer able to distinguish between our thoughts and reality.

A conviction about a certain strategy can blind a leader to other possibilities needed to compensate for changing economic currents. This blind spot can cause serious miscalculations, wasting millions of dollars on faulty strategies. Sometimes the damage is so serious the company is lost; other times, it can take years to recover.

Transcending comparative thought is of strategic importance. Most managers rearrange a company's systems, procedures and structures (which are an outcome of unhealthy thinking) before they deal with the cause—the thinking of the leaders and the team.

Leading From Integrative Presence

As I said earlier, **from moment to moment we are living our thoughts about life, life itself or some combination of both.** What are the differences between life itself and our thoughts about life?

The main problem with comparative thought occurs when we feel these thoughts represent reality as opposed to our thinking about reality. As previously noted, a leader who tends to be a "negative thinker" is caught up in thoughts that create stress, frustration or anger. Decisions influenced by these emotions may not be in the best interest of the business. A strongly held conviction about a certain strategic direction might prevent insight into an even more effective direction. How then, as leaders, do we reduce our cognitive distortions and make decisions closer to the reality of a given business situation?

When leaders report their experiences of Integrative Presence, there is very little comparative thought. They report a clear, peaceful focus, a slow motion effect, the feeling of ease and grace. Exhilaration and a sense of purpose are experienced resulting in extraordinary performance. Why? The answer is that, in Integrative Presence, we have shifted from comparative thought, which is habitual in our culture, to living closer to the moment.

Integrative Presence, because of its lack of linear comparison, is closer to **the reality of the moment.** The Life Force, or the Great Intelligence, is combined with the person's knowledge and training. Integrative Presence is closer to life itself, therefore, more effective in situations where high levels of performance are required.

A basketball player does not have time to think comparatively before he/she makes a cut to the basket. The player can't stop and reflect comparatively…"should I go to the right or left…maybe I should shoot from here…no, there is no time." Business leaders in boardrooms, after making all the presentations and hearing all the feedback and varying points of view, have to make a decision in the moment.

Many athletes remain in the game, long after their bodies are worn out, due to their love of two things: the feeling of being on a team and the experience of being in the moment. Because we are closer to life itself in the moment, we long to repeat the experience. It has been proven that Integrative Presence is not isolated to sports. One can experience this state of mind during any endeavor that one is totally involved with. One can experience this state building a business, creating a new product, solving an important problem or interacting with people.

Integrative Presence creates significant improvement in results and happiness.

A business leader must master the use of thought and understand human nature to create new market and business realities, if they are to stay ahead of the competition.

Remember you cannot create what you cannot conceive; and what you or your team thinks will become manifest.

It is the Mix That Counts

It is the way we mix the Life Force, Consciousness and Thought that counts. Different states of mind come as a result of how we balance these elements in our life.

Using the anorexic persona as an example, it is clear that their state of mind is distorted. But what is happening? The following illustrates:

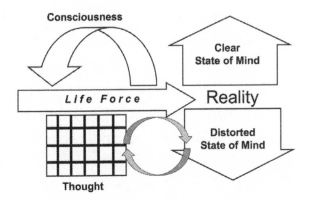

It is as though the Life Force and their level of consciousness are completely blocked out by their thoughts.

They are only conscious of the reality their thoughts create, and that reality is not an accurate or pleasant one. There is no balance between the three elements. Thoughts circle on themselves, and the distortion seems more and more real. This is an extreme example, but we all, to some extent, distort reality with overuse of thought. When a person is experiencing Integrative Presence, their field of consciousness widens. Some say, "It seems like he has eyes in the back of his head." Those in stress, because of overuse of comparative thought on the other hand, have a narrowing field of consciousness. As the foregoing illustrates, the overuse of thought is filtering out their consciousness and their connection to the intelligence.

How Do You Know When it is Right?

While leading a business, it is important not to have an overly distorted view of market trends, people or strategic opportunities. It is important to validate your assumptions with research and data, but statistics can be distorted when a strong thought process is guiding the research. Even good data can be misunderstood by a leader who is distorting the interpretation of the data by strongly held beliefs. After all, the Nazi's had considerable data to prove that they were superior to other races.

People explain that when they are in Integrative Presence they feel peaceful, confident, strong, creative, exhilarated, calm, have a clear view of reality, and respond without thought to the moment. While people who are stressed report that they cannot stop their thinking about the same things over and over again. The first is someone who you might say is in a great mood, and the second is someone in a real bad mood.

The Research

In the book, which was a groundbreaking new approach to happiness, *Sanity, Insanity, and Common Sense,* the authors describe higher and lower mood states in the following manner:

Higher Levels of Consciousness		Lower Levels of Consciousness	
High Mood States			*Low Mood States*
Love, Appreciation, Generosity, Kindness, Gratitude, Compassio,n Patience, Understanding, Creativity, Insight, Sense of Humor, Satisfaction, Contentment,Security, Self-Esteem,Cooperation, Flexibility, Responsibility, Motivation, Interest, Ability to Concentrate, Productivity	**Unconditioned States of Mind:** Wisdom Common Sense Mental Health	**Conditioned States of Mind:**	Achievement, Motivation, Competition, Self-Image, Ego Need to Prove Self, Mental Struggle, Confusion, Seriousness, Commiseration, Impatience, Frustration, Hurriedness, Boredom, Restlessness, Anger, Dissatisfaction, Hate, Defensiveness, Prejudice, Conflict, Paranoia, Misunderstandings, Effort, Drudgery, Incompatibility, Blame, Judgment, Self Righteousness, Stress, Burnout, Anxiety, Inefficiency, Emotional Instability, Sadness, Sorrow, Depression, Hostility, Revenge,

They point out that the lower levels of consciousness are conditioned states of mind that come from thoughts and beliefs that are created by our language and societal norms. These states of mind are based on comparison and distort reality.

By contrast, the higher levels of consciousness are considered unconditioned states of mind that come naturally. These higher levels of consciousness are exhibited when one is in Integrative Presence. It is natural to be in these states, as is indicated by Florence Joyner explaining that her burst of speed comes from "letting go."

Don Ross, CEO and Chairman of New York Life, after saving billions of dollars said, "You have to know the difference between feelings that come from your ego and fear (conditioned states of mind) and those that come from wisdom and common sense." I think the foregoing chart will help you make those distinctions.

Attachment vs. Engagement

What leaders and all people strive for is to live more often in a higher state of mind. The following examples have helped me live more often in Integrative Presence. Lower states of mind are the result of not letting go of comparative thoughts; or to say it in another way, becoming attached to conditioned or repetitive thoughts which block the flow of life.

Using two scales, the following illustrates how we become trapped, or live in Integrative Presence. The first scale is what we call "Engagement" or being connected with the Life Force, being totally involved in the moment and committed to the activity in which you are participating.

The second scale is "Attachment." This means particularly attachment to comparative thoughts or beliefs that are conditioned from the past. We all have various combinations of both attachment and engagement. The following chart illustrates this dynamic:

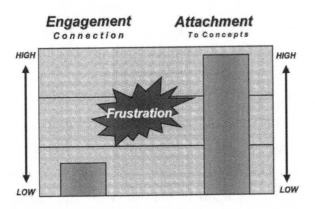

When you have a high level of attachment to achieving something, but a low level of engagement, you naturally feel frustrated. An example would be someone who wants to get married, but refuses to meet people. They stay home and wish someone would find them and carry them away, but it never happens so they feel frustrated. Another example is someone who really wants to be happy, but is never connected to life or activities that stimulate life.

An example in business might be a leader who is committed to a strategy, but does not take the time to describe that strategy. He might hold it in his head and wonder why the team does not understand the correct direction. He is attached to achieving the strategy, but is not engaged with the team in his company or the market place. That leader becomes frustrated with his team, and they do not know why.

When working with a high-tech company, we conducted a survey of management to determine if they understood our strategy. The survey came out very poorly. At the executive staff meeting, the CEO said in disgust, "If they don't understand it by now, they never will. I am not going to waste anymore time communicating this strategy to these people."

I had to be the one to stand up and call a time out. I said, "It is our job as senior leaders in a public company to engage with management in a way that they understand the strategy." I went on to explain that the survey merely gave us a line of sight to how it was not getting through, and that it was our job to find a way to have full engagement with the team.

Another example would be someone who is neither attached nor engaged.

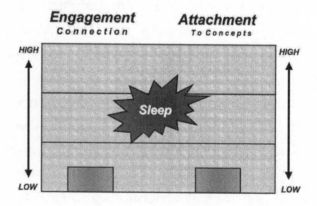

A hippie hiding out in a commune, full of people who just smoke pot and do nothing, would be an example. They really don't care about anything and are not engaged in any activities. They are, in effect, asleep. Not present, but not frustrated either. Company employees can fall into this trap without good leadership. They have gotten no rewards for trying, and so they do not care anymore, and try to get away with the minimum. Leaders who fall into this state, stop being engaged with the business. They might take up golf or boating, and avoid coming into the office. They are neither engaged with the business nor attached to its success or failure. Hopefully, someone within the company will step up to the plate.

Many "A" types, thinking they are maximizing their performance, are both engaged and attached to the outcomes. They suffer from stress and heart attacks, but are so committed that they just keep pushing.

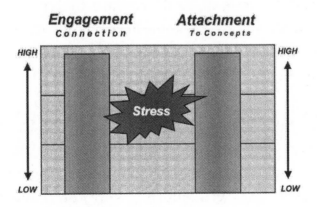

What happens over time is that their level of stress begins to interfere with their engagement, and they become angry and frustrated.

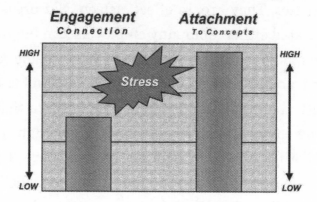

The stress reduces their level of engagement, and their results suffer.

This is hard for many to imagine. For example, let's say two players face each other at a tennis championship. Player "A" is the reigning champion. He has won before and there is no real pressure to win. Player "B," on the other hand, has never won, and the media is making a big deal about this match. They say, if he does not win, he will be finished. Player "B" takes these reports seriously, and is thinking about these reports between shots. Both are equally matched in terms of skills and physical ability. The stress from these thoughts will reduce player "B's" level of engagement, and player "A" will more likely be experiencing "Integrative Presence."

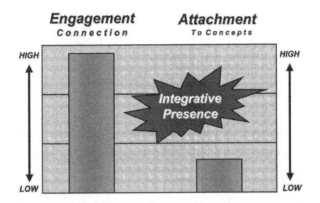

Player "A" will win. He is totally engaged in the game, watching the ball come at him and striking it with no attachment to fear-based thoughts. Like Florence Joyner, he has let go and is totally present. His consciousness is wider and deeper, and he moves with grace and ease. That is why it is so hard to unseat a champion.

The conditioned states of mind are created by comparative thoughts and tend to circle on themselves, drawing the person away from the reality of the moment into conceptual frameworks. Results falter and stimulate more comparative thoughts. The repetition of these thoughts creates stress and other lower levels of consciousness.

Original Thought

Letting go of these kinds of thoughts unleashes genius and results in higher states of mind. It seems from all research that, if the source of your thinking is a high level of consciousness and includes the wisdom that comes from "The Great Intelligence," your thoughts will flow and be of a much higher quality. They will be less distorted and more based in reality. As a leader, it is important that your thoughts come from these high levels of consciousness. To win in the competitive world, you need original thought, not recycled, conditioned thought.

To summarize a great deal of research: **don't make decisions if you are in a bad mood.** Use only thoughts and insights that come from Integrative Presence. Surely the founders of the United States were connected with this wisdom when they wrote the constitution declaring that "all men are created equal." When Microsoft Corporation, a software company that made no computers, said their vision was to have "a computer in every home," this meant they would have to create user friendly software to make that possible.

As I said earlier, "thought precedes manifestation." The question is, what is the quality of your thought? Will the people in your company and market place follow you and the thoughts you create? Are those thoughts based on connection with reality, or are they conditioned patterns that come from thoughts and beliefs you have accepted or were created by someone else? Only original thought will create new realities.

The keys to understanding thought are:

- Thought is a tool to create, not reality
- Thought can trap us in false realities and destroy our lives and business
- Thought is both the greatest gift and the greatest danger in life
- Thought that comes from connection with wisdom is true genius
- Don't take your thoughts too seriously, reality is continuously changing, and thoughts tend to remain the same
- Learn to let go of your recycled thoughts to make room for original thoughts

CONNECTIVITY

In 1964 John Bell showed that the world according to quantum mechanics really is non-local. The universe is non-local at the level of individual events.

As the days get longer and the light from the sun warms up the Earth, tiny green plants start to climb out of the soil and fresh green leaves begin to unfold on the trees. The tribe knows the fresh fruit is not far behind and that young deer will make easy prey. They know the cold has blown its last storm and that the Earth is going to swell with abundance. So they prepare for the gathering and the hunting. They scout the herds and the fields, and wait for nature's full bloom to extend itself.

They know from experience, and can sense through connectivity, the events unfolding; and with precision, they will harvest the spring fruit and plant the crops to grow through the summer.

The Shaman of the Tribe knows when to plant the seeds early enough to achieve maximum growth, but not so early as to be destroyed by a spring frost, which is different every year. Likewise, leaders of global corporations know when to begin the new direction or launch an innovative product just before the competition, but not before the market places are ready.

The Shaman smells the air and feels the Earth, but on some level he just knows. He has become so connected to nature that what might not seem obvious to us is plain as day to him. Great leaders are connected to their customers, to innovative research, to the very flow of patterns that extend themselves across the globe, in the media, and around the water cooler; as the Shaman, they just know. It is due to connectivity, not magic.

The Mathematical Hypothesis

Leaders experiencing Integrative Presence seem to be connected to something beyond them. They are using high levels of consciousness to combine the "Great Intelligence" with their personal wisdom and knowledge. This connectivity was scientifically discovered and proven empirically only within the last twenty years.

In 1964, John Bell showed that the world according to quantum mechanics really is non-local. The universe is non-local at the level of individual events.

*"What actually happens is that a non-locally, **self-referencing web of interrelationships persists and develops**, characterized by a high degree of correlation imposed by symmetry—Imposed correlations like this (which are ubiquitous since all physical systems have*

momentum-energy relationships with other systems)
constitute continuous formative constraints on the
evolution of the universe."

Prior to this mathematical discovery, many philosophers observed that there are three basic elements to life:

- The observer
- The observed
- Invisible connections that flow between them

As illustrated below, these three elements are interdependent as Bell postulated.

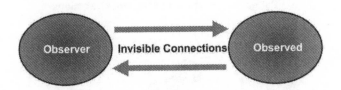

There is an invisible natural intelligence that links things.

Therefore, if this is true with our relationship with the Great Intelligence and each other, you can see how someone experiencing Integrative Presence can perform incredible feats. They are learning from this "self-referencing web of interrelationships" while affecting them with their intention in the moment.

The Proof of Bell's Theorem

While most philosophers and scientists believed this to be true, and anyone who has experienced this state can feel this truth, it was not proven until 1982 when Alain Aspect conducted actual experiments.

"... proving that elementary particles are affected by connections that exist unseen across time and space."
—(Gribbin 1984, 227ff)

Local and non-local connectivity have become facts of physics. What Alain Aspect discovered was that paired electrons in an atom spin in opposite directions. He further proved that if you change the spin on the first electron, the second would change conversely.

Paired Electrons Spin in Opposite Directions

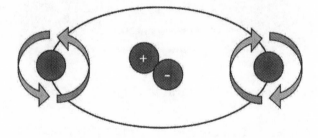

When you change the spin of one, the other changes instantly,
(even separated from the nucleus of the atom).

He then separated these electrons to determine at what distance this effect would continue. He found that the distance did not seem to matter and more important that there was no passing of time over this distance. The effect acted in a non-local manner as Bell had suggested.

Therefore, some intelligence transcends time and space...

No Passage
Of Time

and is at work between all things and at any distance.

The Wisdom Traditions Knew

By 1984, the scientific world believed about connectivity what most philosophers and prophets recognized from their experience of life. It may explain the incredible feats of architecture around the world; the Mayan calendar, which is more accurate than ours; Stonehenge, and other wonders of the ancient world. We find names for this in every tradition around the world.

"The Great Intelligence"—Emerson
"Amazing Grace"—Christianity
"The Source"—Kabala (Judaism)
"The Great Spirit"—American Indian
"The Flow of Heaven"—Taoism

If this intelligence connects everything and allows us to see the true nature of things, then why do we get so disconnected? As the circular arrows below indicate, cognitive distortions interrupt this naturally clear view with beliefs, assumptions, and conditioned cognitive frameworks. It is like the atmosphere of the Earth distorting the light of the stars and making them appear to twinkle, but much less pleasant.

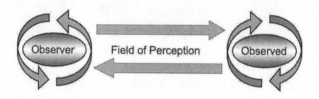

A Teacher's Story

It is possible to travel along these connective fields of perception and see through the personalities that obscure inner genius. These connections are more real than the personalities that are formed by conditioned thought. For example, I know a teacher who is known for her ability to work with emotionally disturbed children. As she walked into the room, the children were bouncing off the walls. As you might imagine, it is very difficult to control a room full of these kinds of children. Based on reports from a number of people, I discovered that she would calm the room in a short period of time when others had given up.

I asked her how she accomplished these incredible feats. She said that she could see each child's inner health and that she would only address that health. She would not answer questions that came from their disturbed personalities. She said she just ignored these actions and focused on the child's inner health. Gradually, the children would begin to see their own health through her eyes and they would start to operate from this healthy place instead of their distorted personalities.

Connectivity is A Primal Need

A mother is deeply connected to her child because that child came from within her. The connection between a mother and a child is one of the deepest forms of love. Examine those you love the most. What is the nature of this love? I suggest that there is a direct relationship between the depth of connection and the strength of that love.

Being connected is a primal need that goes beyond logic. To be banished from the tribe in early history meant a slow death by starvation. Being part of the tribe was essential for survival and remains today as a central motivator for all people. If children do not feel strongly connected to their family, they will find another tribe, perhaps a gang or a social click. A great leader finds ways to deepen the connection between the people on the team, customers, and the market place. It creates loyalty, security, and at the deepest level, love.

Inner Wisdom

People have inner wisdom and beauty because they are connected with the "Great Intelligence" whether they are conscious of it or not. The evidence is the great athletes as they let go and slip into the zone. The evidence is Bell's theorem and your own experience of life at times when you felt connected. People are only using a small percentage of their abilities. As a leader or a friend, the greatest thing you can do for people is to free them from their own limitations and distortions.

Connectivity is why intuition works. Don Ross could know that the market was going to crash. He could feel it through the connective fields that Bell discovered. The animals could feel the tsunami coming along these fields. You can know the flow of your market place by being connected, and people will follow the leader who connects with them.

A Connected Leader

In the late 1990's I was working with the CEO and the executive team of a large hi-tech company. The company had five different business units headed up by an EVP and General Manager. Our intention was to spin off several of these businesses. Out of 9,000 employees, 4,500 had PhD's, and there were many "Double Es." We had three production facilities, and close to 7,000 of the 9,000 people were engineers. The key to success was product innovation and speed to market. Leadership required high levels of technical competency and an ability to lead highly educated people. Not a simple task.

I worked with one of the general managers, who led one of the fastest growing businesses. He was both technically astute and an excellent sales leader. He was always able to drive products to market before the competition. He had strong relationships with the company's clients and drove innovation from his office. He had worked his way to the top by being fairly ruthless. His executive staff was always trying to hide problems from him because they feared his wrath. He spent most of his time trying to find out what was really going on, and the staff spent as much time trying to hide. With some encouragement from me and the CEO, he decided to take his team off-site for a three-day leadership and team development process.

During the process, he had to step out of the room for about two hours to participate in an earnings call. The minute he left, his entire senior team approached me with complaints about his behavior. They explained that he was rude, and abusive and that most of them were looking for another job. At that time, good talent was very hard to find. A mass exodus of this kind of talent would have surely destroyed this division and ended our plans to spin it off.

After about an hour of discussion, I said to them that I would certainly work with him, but each of them must take a stand when he is being abusive. You cannot expect that I or the CEO will be able to save you every time something like this occurs. You have to take responsibility for your own state of mind and mental health. They agreed, but still were very upset.

When the General Manager returned from the earnings call, I pulled him aside and explained what had occurred while he was away. While he was concerned at the prospect of losing his team, he explained that he had to be a tough leader, otherwise the team would walk all over him. After much conversation with him making it clear that the CEO was also concerned with his behavior, he said to me, "So what you are telling me is that I need to be less assertive with my team." I said, "No. I want you to continue to be assertive; it is one of your greatest strengths. You have built the business with your vision into market opportunities and the assertive manner in which you have driven your products to market before the competition. What I want you to do is learn to separate assertiveness from abusiveness. The two are not mutually exclusive. You can be assertive without being abusive."

In that moment, he totally understood. I could almost see him letting go of all the beliefs and assumptions that surrounded his inner genius. It was like watching dark clouds blow away from a mountain top to reveal beauty. The cognitive frameworks he had built up connecting assertiveness and abuse began to fall apart. We went back into the room with his team and he apologized for his past behavior. He explained what he had realized in his conversation with me. He promised to work on these behaviors and asked them to alert him should they reoccur. He said he would continue to work with me until he was free of these inappropriate behaviors. You could feel the connection growing between him and his team as he spoke to them that day.

That saved the meeting, but, of course, there was much work to be done over the next year. I helped him, and he became even more successful. When we were getting ready to spin this company off, the CEO wanted me to interview each of his staff to be sure he would be the right person to be CEO of this new company. During the interviews almost all of his staff said that if he were not chosen to be CEO, they would resign. Once he let go of the cognitive framework that created his abusive behaviors, it allowed his team to connect with his genius. He and his team were working in a connected manner, and they had a successful spin off even in the difficult times that followed the 1990's.

Imagine a great leader (perhaps yourself) able to connect with this intelligence, traveling along the connective fields of perception and seeing through peoples' masks into their greatness and inner wisdom. As you connect with people's inner greatness, it draws back the veil of cognition and helps the person see beyond their own distortions. This helps both of you reach a higher level of consciousness. The people on your team are connected to each other and to the "Great Intelligence," mutually expanding each other's wisdom. It is hard to beat a team that is this well-connected.

Remember there is no substitute for practice. Capture your insights and actions steps in your journal.

Key elements for the reader to remember are:

- It has been proven that all things are actually connected
- Distortion of these connections occurs with our beliefs
- Integrative Presence imports information over these connections
- Being connected is a primal need
- Connecting with someone's genius can draw it out
- A leader must have clear connections to the team, the market place and the flow of the intelligence within that market place

EXPANSION

When leaders understand that expanding the human spirit is central to leadership, it profoundly changes the way they lead.

According to discoveries made by the Hubble Telescope, the universe is expanding. The latest discoveries in physics indicate that the Universe itself is a relational network of energy. If this network is expanding, that suggests that the very fabric that makes up human existence is growing in some manner. If this is true, then to try to remain the same is contrary to the laws of the Universe, which of course we are part of. It is no wonder that many philosophers and thought leaders believe that much of human suffering comes from resisting change. Bob Dylan, poet and folk singer, summed these notions up in the simple phrase:

"He who is not busy being born is busy dying."

What does this have to do with leadership? Why should a leader be concerned with the nature of the Universe? The simple answer is that each leader is navigating their organizations through this Universe and is subject to its laws. Anyone who would like to set records for speed in swimming would, of course, want to be swimming down stream as opposed to swimming against the current. Likewise, in business one wants to swim with the currents of the market place. If the current of the universe is expansion, then it would follow that a business that is expanding will thrive; one that tries to remain the same will have to work harder and make less progress, as will the upstream swimmer.

There is a momentum that acts like a current in a river that you can swim with or against. Most leaders have experienced this during periods of success. It seems like you can do nothing wrong; each decision seems obvious and one leads to another, like an athlete "in the zone." During economic growth or slowing, there are correct actions, patterns in the economic flow that, when followed, expand the effectiveness of your business.

All experienced leaders have also experienced swimming upstream. It seems like no matter what you try, it works out wrong. Each decision seems difficult, and one mistake leads to another; you and your team are tired and frustrated, like an athlete full of stress and hesitancy.

Beyond pure physics, it is clear that the world populations, economic systems, knowledge, technology and free market systems are expanding. The world of human endeavor is expanding all over this planet. Is your business swimming in the currents of expansion, or is it caught in an eddy, or worse yet, swimming against the current? To contract or stay the same is against all business, scientific and philosophical principles; it is like swimming upstream in white water.

The purpose of this chapter is to understand the nature of expansion and how to use it to affect your business. For it is clear that a business not busy expanding is busy dying.

Expansion Starts With You

The only way for your business to expand into new markets, to achieve new levels of performance, is to have the teams of people who run your business expand in knowledge and spirit. As the leader of the teams that run your business, you must be the first to expand.

A business does not grow by virtue of a financial need, it grows because the people who run that business, and then the market place, are committed to the expansion of the value proposition that the business represents. *A leader must become master of expanding the spirit of the people who drive the expansion of the business.*

When the human spirit is expanding, individuals are trusting, hopeful, creative, accountable, energized, compassionate, grateful, powerful, understanding and passionate. They rise with grace and ease to any challenge. They are adaptable to a changing environment.

When the human spirit is contracting, individuals are fearful, hopeless, victims, tired, judgmental, selfish, isolated, confused, and resigned. The slightest change irritates and may anger them.

Noticing the difference between these two states of mind in individuals, teams or corporate cultures is not rocket science. You don't need to conduct expensive surveys and analysis. It is clear when an organization is focused on the problem rather than the solution. Low morale takes high levels of denial to miss. However, it is easier to notice a contracting attitude or organizational culture than it is to change that culture.

For example, the performances of centralized economies that have restricted the human spirit and are devoid of feedback systems, such as elections, pale in comparison to free market economies. World Communism failed and the economies based on elitism, caste systems, dictatorships and monarchies have little hope of competing with the free market economies based upon opportunity.

While working with a large financial services company's executive team in the 1980's, I asked them, "Of the two major economic systems in the world, which was the most productive, the USSR or the USA?" Obviously they answered, "The USA." Then I asked, "Why?" They went on to explain we were the land of opportunity, that people were free to create businesses, and that our free market system draws in creative people from all around the world. Conversely, the Soviet Union was centrally controlled and people's spirit was constrained. We in the US often benefited from what was called "the brain drain," as top scientists and artists defected.

I then asked, "Given that the phrase 'no decision is too small for the Executive Management Committee' echoes throughout the halls, which of the two systems does this company most resemble?" In that moment, insight occurred. The CEO and Executive Team realized that, if they were to become truly competitive and expand their business beyond its present state, something had to change. This need to control everything from the top was constricting the human spirit and the development of products. They were consistently late to market with products. Often competitors would have products on the market before proposals even reached the Executive Management Committee.

As they realized the folly of the cognitive frameworks that were constraining the genius of the company, they started to let go of unnecessary processes. They created semi-independent business units, put their leaders through a leadership and team development process similar to the one they experienced themselves, and became a truly dynamic company.

This company was not intentionally constricting the human spirit. They had formed habits and traditions that worked in the past, but were no longer useful. It is often the case that one or two beliefs like this are constraining the genius of potentially great companies. The trick is to see the company's past genius, connect with them by acknowledging the successes that built the past, and find a way for them to see what belief system is blocking their present success. As always, once unleashed, spirit and genius expands at ever-increasing rates.

Expanding the human spirit, consciousness and unleashing genius is the job of a leader. Once leaders understand that expansion of the human spirit is central to organizational success, it profoundly affects the way they lead. Leaders look for long-term solutions instead of quick fixes. Leaders coach to build people up, instead of criticize. Leaders are accountable for the success of the entire organization, instead of meeting the needs of narrow interest groups. Leaders are trusted and followed because of who they are, instead of complied with, in fear of what they might do.

The best leaders are skilled in seeing each person's genius and challenging them to manifest that genius. Because as every person grows, so does the business. The great German philosopher agrees:

"If I accept you as you are, I will make you worse; however, if I treat you as though you are what you are capable of becoming, I help you become that."
—Johann Wolfgang von Goethe

A true leader is a champion of the mission and acts to draw out the genius and spirit of the team in a way that the team feels it is their own creation. In the fifth century B.C., Lao Tzu said to the ruler he served:

"A leader is most effective when people barely know he exists. When his work is done, his aim fulfilled, his troops will feel they did it themselves."

The power of the human spirit can be expanded in a number of ways, all of which we will discuss in this chapter. Essentially, the enemy of all leaders is selfishness, which creates contraction; the friend is commitment, which creates expansion. Commitment to something larger than self is particularly effective for unleashing this robust power.

The Problem

It is clear that people resist change and even struggle to prevent any kind of expansion beyond what they are "used to." Every leader has experienced this resistance. Why then, if expansion surrounds us and is the very fabric of our universe, do we as humans for the most part fail to expand and, in fact, work hard to maintain the status quo?

Our language is based on comparative thought. We cannot say anything without making a comparison. Even if we say we are neutral, it is opposed to having a point of view. Our language is based on duality. For example: things are good or bad, right or wrong, negative or positive, or neutral or not. Our system of thought is linear, two-dimensional and fairly static. Using this thought system to define an ever-expanding universe can cause problems.

Additionally, comparative thought, when combined with our level of consciousness, creates psychological realities which may not be real, that we tend to cling to like life and death. In business, if we cling to the wrong realities, it can be the death of our business.

As I explained earlier, attachment to a thought or belief system can prevent full engagement in the reality of the moment. The more attached a leader is to a cognitive framework, the more blinded that leader will be to what is really occurring, which is more likely some kind of expansion or change in direction that will lead to expansion of the market place. The problem with unsuccessful companies is that they get attached and locked into a framework that is not in touch with the reality of the moment.

Why We Resist and Fear Change

Our behaviors as leaders are driven by our beliefs and assumptions which are formed from past experiences. We approach the field of present experience from, what behavioral scientists call a "belief system." This is everyone's unique combination of beliefs and assumptions that form our personalities, control our perception, and develop our leadership style.

The Habit Cycle

A belief system is made up of conscious and unconscious beliefs that drive our behavior. The following graphic illustrates how we learn habits, and then tend to repeat them. Some experiences are so strong that they drive us into insight and reflection. From that insight and reflection, we form a belief or assumption that in turn drives our behaviors and actions. Unfortunately, once a behavior pattern is established, it tends to repeat itself (**"Habit Cycle"**), unless interrupted by a consequence or experience powerful enough to cause deep reflection within the **"Learning Cycle"** which changes the beliefs and assumptions that have driven that behavior.

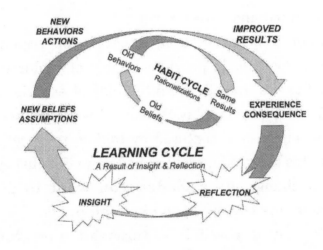

It is important to note here that all beliefs that drive our behavior are not necessarily conscious. **Many beliefs are totally unconscious.** These unconscious beliefs are often in conflict with our conscious beliefs. A person may consciously believe in a change, but due to an unconscious belief that sounds something like, "If it works, don't fix it...we have always done it this way," that person will find themselves doing things to resist change. People around that person will see these behaviors, but the person cannot see their own limiting behaviors and will attribute them to bad luck, other people's problems, etc.

Organizations are a collection of conscious and unconscious belief systems. Often the conscious, or stated beliefs, are in conflict with the unconscious beliefs. This is why a corporation can have a conscious belief to change and expand while most people in the corporation **do not really believe it will happen,** the result being something less than the stated and agreed upon goal.

Without a belief system, a person or organization could not operate. It provides a way of understanding and sorting the literally infinite fields of experience that are in front of us every day. Without this system, we would be overwhelmed and confused by taking in everything at once. That is the good news. The bad news is, belief systems can limit change. **As a leader, you want to develop belief systems that lead to expansion.**

We look at all possibilities through the programming of past events which influences our choices in the present. All your employees have established a matrix of belief systems regarding your existing strategy, and will have a hard time seeing the new strategy. The following is a classic tool used by psychologists, which you have probably seen, which illustrates.

Lock-in/Lock-out:

Do you see the old lady or the young lady?

Once your mind selects one or the other of the two images on this drawing, it stops looking for the second. Humans have a deep need to be right, so they lock-in once they discover something familiar and stop looking for alternatives.

The same is true with cultural habits and norms. Once your team forms these habits, the only way to unlock them from bad habits and lock them into good habits is through professional intervention. If you hope to have them see the young lady, or new culture, it will take work.

Emotional Cycle of Change

Even when you have worked hard to have your team see a new way of doing things, most people go through what is called the **"Emotional Cycle of Change."** No matter how positive the change or how committed the person is to that change, the following cycle seems to be inevitable.

As pictured on the following graphic, we all start with a high level of **uninformed optimism** at the beginning of any change. As we begin to face the reality *of* making changes in deeply rooted habits, our level of optimism begins to sink. When levels of optimism drop, most people **give up and return to old habits,** even though they know those old habits have little benefit. The immediate discomfort of changing habits, and fear of the unknown, seems to overwhelm the long-term benefits of change.

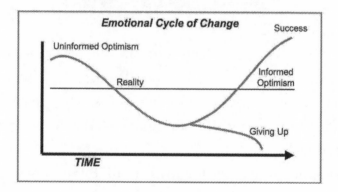

People who have consistent success implementing change in their lives have high levels of **determination and commitment** that lead them through low levels of optimism to **informed optimism and success.** Once people have persisted through "reality" and succeeded, the change is permanent. The following are some of the keys to achieving success:

1. Recognize that change is difficult and be prepared for this "reality"
2. Understand that all people, no matter how successful, go through this cycle
3. See sinking optimism as a challenge and a natural phase to success
4. Clearly describe the change and review it daily
5. Describe the pain or negative outcomes of not succeeding and review daily
6. Describe the pleasure or positive outcomes of succeeding and review daily
7. Be willing to change your methods of creating change
8. Never surrender; never give up, until you have success

Imagine what it will be like being part of this team if we all succeed in making the changes we have committed to. How will it be different? Ask yourself: will it be worth the pain of stepping outside of our "Zone of Comfort" and venturing into the unknown?

Reprogramming

Great athletes and teams know that there is always room for improvement. New records are set year after year. **Each new record requires massive changes in the athlete's body and practices,** which causes expansion of their abilities and endurance. To increase strength and endurance, you have to push through the body's natural resistance. As your abilities expand, you start to feel exhilarated. This is because your expansion matches the natural state of the universe you live within.

All those who have left a trail of greatness are busy expanding their consciousness and abilities, because they know that without expansion, others will pass them by, and, of course, this is also true for corporations.

Certain experiences seem to accelerate expansion. When the accepted limits of performance are broken, improvements and discoveries spread at increased rates. For example: at one time no one believed a man could run the mile in less than four minutes, fly faster than the speed of sound, or walk on the moon.

Breaking these barriers created new realities and accelerated performance in running, aviation and technology. Once these records were broken, the world had a living vision for the possibility. Within the first year after the "four minute mile" was broken, over three hundred athletes broke the "four minute mile."

Most business organizations have strong beliefs about what seem to be impossible barriers: growing while maintaining that special feeling that first created success, reducing costs again, increasing profits or taking market share from a dominant competitor. The reason for this is that it is hard to conceive of performance levels never experienced, or find events that open people to the possibility of dramatic performance improvements.

The question is: what experiences create enough insight and reflection to stimulate an

organization to commit to changes that they have never experienced before? The draw of habit, or our comfort zone, combines with human kind's natural fear of the unknown. These two factors are the major reasons people refuse to change:

- Habit and comfort
- Fear of the unknown

In Roger Banister's day, the world believed that no human could run the mile in less than four minutes. Doctors had written in medical journals that it was physically impossible. They theorized that your heart would burst or your eyes would pop out. These beliefs provided little incentive to break the habit of pacing under four minutes, and great fear of the unknown after four minutes.

In a moment of reflection and insight, Roger Banister stopped after completing a quarter mile without being winded and said to his team mates, "I can put four of these together." The experience enabled him to see beyond accepted limits, and suddenly he saw a vision he could commit to. **The fear and darkness of the unknown was filled up with his vision.** He declared his commitment, realized he needed more stamina, set up an aggressive conditioning schedule, practiced for over a year before succeeding, and finally the vision he saw that day became a reality.

The hard work of practice did not come until he had an insight, which as defined earlier, is: "Seeing into the true nature of something." He could see "in the moment" that all the beliefs and assumptions of society were not true. He saw the true nature of human ability. He conceived a future possibility that filled the unknown with light.

When the accepted limits of human performance are broken, it releases waves of energy and improved perform-ance. Now, you will probably not make the high school track team if you cannot run a mile under four minutes. As leader of a corporation, breaking through accepted limits and creating waves of improved performance is critical to success.

The Black Box of Culture

There are many reasons that lead to 70% of mergers and acquisitions failing to reach their stated goals, and the fact that most strategies and initiatives are not implemented suc-cessfully. One of the big reasons for this is what's called "The Black Box of Culture." Every organization has a culture, which in its simplest form is **"the way we do things around here,"** as was illustrated earlier with the phrase "no decision is too small for the Executive Management Committee." The way we do things around here is defined in more detail by the organizational values and beliefs. These values and beliefs form a type of software that is often hidden. But the software that forms a network of beliefs and assumptions determines people's behaviors, which in turn determine results. If a leader does not reprogram these beliefs and assumptions, as Roger Banister did, the organization's performance will not expand.

The organization or team will continue to believe either unconsciously or consciously that there are certain limits, and their behavior will be the same as always, thus producing similar results. The following illustrates:

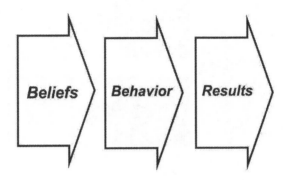

Every strategic initiative must pass through "The Black Box of Culture," which is formed by a matrix of beliefs and assumptions that are locked-in, while the possibility of future expansion is locked-out.

When I was working with a railroad company, the predominant belief at the time was that their railroad was the greatest railroad in the world. It was disloyal to express any other view. This was the foundation of their organizational culture. While positive beliefs are nice, if they are not true, they can block expansion.

I did some research through some of my associates on Wall Street, and found that one of the key indicators of success in this business was asset utilization. For a railroad at that time, 100% utilization was created by always hauling one hundred railroad cars. Anything short of that would not be full utilization. Their utilization was below average. But the culture blinded them to this reality.

Black Box of Culture

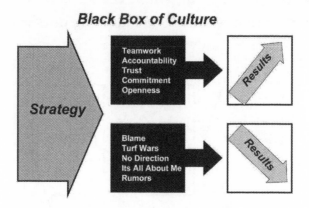

I asked the CFO what it would mean financially if their asset utilization was at average instead of below average. He said it would contribute 375 million dollars to the bottom line each year.

This railroad tracked the engines and the railroad cars in real time. They knew where every car was and could view their location in a massive control room. So I wondered why they could not arrange things to improve this utilization. The answer was not technology; it was "The Black Box of Culture." The head of operations and the head of sales and marketing were at war with each other, and had been for years. As a result, so were the teams that followed each of them.

Each of the teams worked to make the other fail, and the result was often railroad cars full of freight did not get pulled on time, or pulled to maximize utilization. There was very little teamwork and lots of blaming and finger pointing. The result was at least a loss of 375 million dollars each year by having below average utilization. They had the computer system that could put them on top, and the improvements would yield many more millions.

These executives were locked-in to beliefs that had nothing to do with building a successful business on one hand, while on the other hand believing they were running the greatest railroad in the world. Once I facilitated insight into this problem, the entire team pulled together with the help of the new CEO to get these two executives on the same team, and to move towards becoming a truly great railroad. Often there are one or two beliefs that restrain the expansion of a business. As a leader, if you can discover these and create insight that releases people from their grip, you can truly unleash genius.

The leader must find ways to create insight, like Roger Banister had while standing on the track that day realizing he could "put four of these together"; then act on that insight in ways that cause people to put in the work that will expand performance. Once a small example of a break-through performance occurs, the leader must communicate this success, as did the press in Roger Banister's day.

When I was working for Senn-Delaney Leadership Consulting to help reengineer retail stores early in my career, we found the best way to expand the consciousness of those running stores in the old way, was to choose two or three model stores. We would select stores that were lead by people who were naturally open to change, and then spend the time working with the people in the model store to create a true openness to change. We combined our ideas with theirs and created a new reality in store performance, which we tested and fine tuned over time.

Each model store would get our 100% attention. We would implement the new way, lead the team through their natural resistance to change, and prove the case for the new way. We would implement methods and approaches, test them, fine-tune them, until the stores were naturally producing greater results.

We would then launch a publicity campaign with testimonials from model store employees and leaders. The stories would be captured on video and played at Store Manager meetings. Informally, the word would leak out, with a little help from our team. We found people in the 2000 other stores would be asking, "When are we going to get the "New Way." Others would say, "Why do we have to wait so long?" When this level of insight began to expand throughout the chain, not a moment before, we would begin the roll-out of the "New Way" to all the stores. Metaphorically, the 4-minute mile was broken.

First, we created insight and expansion of consciousness on a micro level, and then leveraged that insight to the macro level. We always started small and bridged to the larger picture.

Before we developed this method, many retail chains created disasters for themselves by trying to roll-out a new way to the entire chain before fine-tuning and proving the case at a local level. The result was always failure. Making adjustments and fine-tuning over 2000 stores and thousands of people would be very expensive and slow, but worse was the contraction of morale and belief in the "New Way." The pain of massive implementation, unattended by expert change agents, would destroy people's hope in the "New Way" and those that were leading the change. In fact as Bob Dylan might have said, "They were busy dying." Whereas those retail chains who practiced the art of creating insight that lead to expansion of consciousness were, "Busy being born."

However, as you can see by the preceding examples, it is very difficult to break out of habits and limit expansion. Throughout this book, I am asking you to examine times in your life when you experienced, if only for an hour, when you were expanding. Doing these exercises will help you know how it feels and understand the structure and strategy on a small scale, before you expand the practice throughout your life.

Life, business and the universe we live in are clearly not two-dimensional. Successful leaders have learned to master more than the two dimensions that our language is based upon. They get a feel for things on a small scale in a multi-dimensional manner and then expand that into the rest of their lives. A Ph.D. psychologist/surfer from Harvard, who came to California to work and surf, explained that you cannot think your way into a wave. She said, "You have to feel your way into the wave." The exercises in the *Unleashing Genius Insight and Action Steps Journal* are designed to help you feel your way into new levels of understanding. Again, please take the time to rigorously practice these exercises!

Key concepts and understandings are:
- You are either expanding or contracting
- If you and your team do not expand knowledge, wisdom and consciousness, the business you are leading will not expand
- Problems cannot be solved at the same level of thinking that created them
- People resist change with all their heart and soul
- You must move people through "The Emotional Cycle of Change"
- Unleashing genius creates natural expansion and creativity
- How to unleash genius within the organization

POWERFUL VISION

You are your vision and everything before "but" does not count.

In prehistoric times, under the full moon, moving through the flickering light to the sound of drums and the crackle of the flames, the hunters, dressed as hunter and prey, would dance around the roaring fire acting out the hunt in a ceremonial passion play. They set their intention, educated younger hunters, got permission from the huntress goddess of the moon, and provided a clear vision and purpose for the next day. The entire community gathered to be part of the magical dance that lifted the spirits of the hunters and moved providence.

Thousands of years before the written word, our ancestor's enacted visions of success before the hunt, passed down stories of success around the fire, and recorded these visions on the walls of their caves to provide a clear picture of success for generations to come. Survival of our ancestors depended on a clear understanding of these skills.

So too do modern organizations need clear visions to capture market share. Having a clear vision of the future, support of the community, and a passion to succeed, precedes the written word. It is so deeply woven into the fabric of humanity that, without it, people become lost, fearful and scattered.

The greatest leaders extend the patterns of the present to see strategic windows of opportunity, and crystallize these opportunities into visions, missions and value propositions that guide the members of their organization in the correct direction. They recognize that *you cannot create what you can't conceive,* so they create multiple ways to conceptualize the behaviors and actions that will lead to success.

Strategic Window of Opportunity

An organization's strategic window of opportunity is open when its strengths meet customer requirements and highlight the competition's weaknesses. However, this opportunity, though it may be real, requires imagination to conceive.

One of the great thinkers of our time said,

"Imagination is more important than knowledge."
—*Albert Einstein*

The leader must be able to conceptualize and describe the entire picture of how the team will rocket through the strategic window of opportunity before the competition. Once a leader sees this opportunity, it is his or her job to communicate it in a way that creates a great sense of urgency and commitment on the part of the team, as powerful as the commitment of the hunters of prehistoric times.

This vision should include the mission, strategies, culture, state of the competition, flow of the marketplace, and rewards for success. The most successful leaders can visualize these opportunities clearly and communicate them in a clear and compelling manner.

Phil Jackson, one of the most successful professional basketball coaches of our time said:

"Visualization is the bridge I use to link the grand vision of the team I conjure up every summer to the evolving reality of the court. That vision becomes a working sketch that I adjust, refine and sometimes scrap altogether as the season develops"
—*Phil Jackson, Sacred Hoops (1995)*

You Are Your Vision...Everything before "But" Doesn't Count

All organizations have stated Vision, Mission, Strategies and Organizational Culture, and hopefully they are correct.

However, often times those that are stated are not in fact the same as the organization's collective perceived reality.

The "Water Ball" or the Green?

A story best illustrates. Once I was golfing with my younger brother, who is a golf professional. I was getting ready to hit my ball off the tee on a par three hole. There was a big lake between the green and me. Just as I was about to swing, my brother pointed to my ball and said, "What is that?"

I said, "My ball."

He said, "What kind of ball?"

I picked it up, and in a condescending manner, read the name on the ball and said, "Titlest."

He explained: "That is not the ball you used on the last hole; what nickname might you give this old beat up ball you are about to hit?"

I said, "My water ball."

"I see," he said. "Are you planning on hitting the ball in the water?"

"No," I replied, "but most of the time my ball goes into the water and I do not want to waste a good ball."

"So your vision is the water?" he asked.

I replied, "No."

He asked, "If I did a scan of your brain what kind of images would fill it—images about the water or the green?"

I replied, "The water...how to avoid the water...don't go in the water again...etc."

He then went on to explain that his head contained nothing but the green and the pin placement. He never goes in the water.

Of course, I hit my brand new ball in the water just to be right about using my water ball. But the point is that successful people and organizations put all their energy and focus on their vision for the future.

What is Your True Vision?

The green for your organization is your vision, mission, strategies and culture. The vision, mission, strategies and culture could become considerations and "buts" that follow our formal statements. For example: "Customer Intimacy" may be the vision for one of your written strategies, but the actual vision may sound more like this:

"We need Customer Intimacy, **but** *we don't have the time to be spending on these kinds of things. Besides, as long as we have the best products they will come to us. We can't even predict delivery schedules. I practice Customer Intimacy,* **but** *engineers don't care about this soft stuff."*

Whatever defines your cultural attitudes and beliefs is your true vision for your strategy. When people are more committed to their considerations than their vision, the organization will become the considerations. To know what your real vision is at any time, we need only to look at the present state of your organization.

Do the present attitudes, beliefs and behaviors support your organizational goals? If not, there is work to be done. Leaders must learn to take a stand when they hear people losing hope and help people see the vision and the possibility of success.

There is a time lag between the vision, its cultural impact, its effect on behaviors and its impact on the bottom-line. If you see behaviors that do not match your vision, then you know there are cultural attitudes driving them. These are leading indicators. If they are negative, they will cause a dip in results. The time to deal with these behaviors and attitudes is before they affect the bottom-line. The following illustrates:

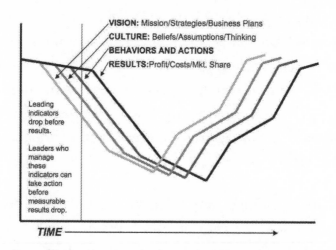

Ask yourself: what is the real strategy for your company? Is it your stated strategy or a bunch of considerations and complaints that are socialized at the water cooler? What can you do to have people around you see your vision, mission, strategies, and culture more clearly? These beliefs will turn into results either negative or positive.

The hunting tribes had no doubt about their vision and all members of those tribes did their part, from the hunters to those that prepared and stored the meat for winter. There were no "buts" in their minds. Success equaled survival, and failure equaled slow death by starvation. Remember, we will become the vision that we "really believe." Do you want the water or the green, economic death or success?

Creating Clear Vision

About 24 years ago I was in a transition period in my life and business career. I had been working as a trouble shooter for a couple of 70's style conglomerates. My last assignment was in California. I became attached to the wonderful weather, and when asked to return to the Northeast, I decided to stay here and look for work.

Several of my friends suggested I take a personal development course they had taken. I was not really interested, but they were so enthused that they volunteered to pay my way.

Upon entering the course, I discovered people from many different walks of life: businessmen, artists, students and people going through divorces. I went along and learned a great deal about myself. Even more important was the epiphany I had at the end of the course.

I was standing in the back of the room watching the facilitator conduct closing ceremonies, when I realized that this group of people had come together as a team, a family and group of colleagues committed to each other's success over the course of five days. Though I knew that in a few weeks we would all become scattered and lose much of the commitment, I could see the power of this kind of work.

At that moment, I realized that I could make this process boardroom friendly and conduct interventions in business that would be much more powerful than what I had done in the past. Unlike a group of people brought together randomly, a business team stays together and can be reinforced.

Saw Myself Leading Business Teams

In that moment I could see myself leading off-sites with business teams and working with them to implement the insights they gained. It was like it had already happened.

I took all the courses this training organization offered and mastered its methodologies and philosophies. In social gatherings, people would actually ask me if I was a consultant or facilitator, and I replied that I would be.

I Was Totally Committed

I began working on course materials and finding opportunities to speak. During a public meeting, after I had spoken, someone approached me.

She said, "Have you met anyone from Senn-Delaney?"

"No," I replied.

Then this woman said, "You need to meet these people."

I asked, "What do they do?"

She said, "They have made the transformational process that you went through boardroom friendly, and they are looking for consultants."

She knew of my involvement in the transformational courses I mentioned earlier. Of course, I wanted to meet these people.

I Declared and Communicated My Intention

Because of the clear vision I had earlier, I said, "I intend to facilitate a transformational business course, and would love to meet these people."

She set the meeting up, and I interviewed with all six people in this new organization.

A Difference between My Vision and Reality

As I began the interview process, I realized that there were a number of skills and crucial background that I didn't have. The President of the company explained to me that I had great business skills, but no real training skills, other than the work that I had done with the transformational organization. He added that most candidates for this job had videos of themselves training.

I interrupted his rejection speech before he had a change to finish and said, "What if I had a video of myself trainingwould you look at it before you made your final decision?" He agreed, leaving me the weekend to produce a video.

Fortunately, a high school friend of mine had come to Hollywood to become a movie actor and had a production studio available.

The Plan Was Set

I gathered all my friends for a weekend project and we staged this transformational seminar with me as the facilitator. We worked through the weekend taking shots that showed my skills and the learning that the participants received. We even did testimonials.

Late Sunday night we had a copy on VHS and it occurred to one of my friends that Senn-Delaney may only have Beta; at the time both were equally popular modes for video tapes. We spent the rest of the night finding equipment to make the Beta copy; I rushed home for a shower and arrived for my final interview.

I Was Ready For Action

I walked into the President's office and he asked if I had brought the video. I smiled and set the VHS copy on his desk. He explained that he would not be able to play it because all of their equipment was Beta. Of course, I reached into my brief case and passed him the Beta version. He was visibly impressed.

He hired me on the spot, and told me later that he was so impressed with my commitment and accountability that he felt he could train me to do anything. I spent 18 wonderful years helping to build this executive development organization, and it all came from the one moment in the back of that training room when I saw myself doing what I am doing today.

I have told this story hundreds of times to have individuals in corporations find a similar story in their life. Each time we analyze the stories, we find the following elements.

Discovering and Implementing Vision

1. *See, feel and hear it in your mind's eye*
2. *Commitment/intention*
3. *Declare and communicate your intention*
4. *Acknowledge the gap between your vision and present reality*
5. *Plan the steps to fill the gap*
6. *Take action with powerful intent*

In every case people started with a powerful and clear vision of succeeding. That vision was a full sensory picture that they could see, hear and feel in their mind's eye. That picture leads to commitment, declaration and a realistic view of reality that guided their plans and actions. It is always the case when a vision has been successfully implemented.

Of course, these steps are not exactly linear, but the first three precede the second three. The work to clarify the vision comes before acknowledging reality. If you develop your vision with barriers or "buts" in mind, the vision will be limited by your beliefs. Work with vision, commitment and communication in the circular manner illustrated below, and then spend the time to acknowledge reality and make plans to fill in the gap.

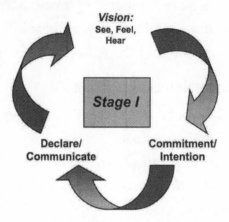

If you do the work in the first stage correctly, you will not have to change the vision when things get tough. You will change the plan as you see the gap between your vision and reality widening.

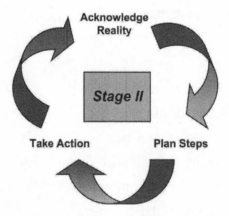

When your team sees you continuously changing the vision or mission, they lose faith in your leadership. False starts create hesitancy because the team will wait to begin action in anticipation of a new "vision of the month." A leader must do the homework in Stage I. In a corporation that means serious strategic thinking, market research and a full analysis of competitive strengths and weaknesses.

Seven Steps to Success

Over the years of work with successful leaders, I have found seven key steps for creating and manifesting vision. These **"Seven Steps"** are the key to **leading people out of the limits of their past beliefs and beyond the fear of the unknown to changes that can set records.** A leader is always asking people not only to accept change, but to go beyond previously established limits. Successful leaders become masters of these steps. The following provides more detail for those who are running an organization.

1. Discover Your Vision

Actively reflect, do research, and talk to people about what you want. Do market research and seek input from many sources as you formulate your ideas. Trust your instincts. Your true vision will be an extension of who you are and it will feel right. It will be a natural extension of you and your organization's genius. You should be able to **see, feel and hear your vision in your mind's eye.** It will be a total sensory experience, as though it has already happened. Roger Banister could see himself running the four-minute mile; he could hear the cheers and was certain of success.

To lead a corporation, a critical mass of the employees must have a clear picture of the corporate vision, mission and strategy, and each employee must understand their role and be passionate about playing on a championship team. Each employee must be committed and articulate about how to win, and view success as inevitable.

2. Total Commitment

If you are not totally committed, then stop and go back to step one. **Commitment will naturally follow as understanding of the vision deepens.** If you want others involved, be sure they understand and are also committed. Build commitment by involving others in fine-tuning the vision and developing ideas for implementation.

The difference between a team committed to winning and one who will try their best is huge. **Accept nothing less than total commitment.** If the team is not totally committed, it is the job of leadership to develop that commitment.

3. Communicate Your Vision

You cannot create something that you cannot conceive and, if you want to involve others in achieving something, then you must be able to communicate in a compelling manner. Prepare compelling written, media, and oral descriptions of your vision, mission and strategy and take the risk of **declaring it to others as something you are absolutely**

going to make happen. Ask for help, feedback and ideas to make it happen. A corporate leader cannot implement a complex strategy alone and will need the help of thousands of people within the organization and market place.

4. Acknowledge Reality

What are the problems? **What is the real difference between your vision and present reality?** Be open to feedback from others! Do not accept your first thoughts, look deeper. Avoid the trap of too much "positive thinking;" you may talk yourself into believing that all you have to do is wait and it will come.

Do research and talk to customers. Be sure your team is capable, and fine-tune the vision until all key leaders are committed and are able to communicate this vision, before developing a plan.

5. Create A Plan

Create a written plan that fills in the gaps between present reality and your vision. Your plan will be more focused and waste less time if you are honest in step four. Your plan should have **key missions and strategies defined by goals and objectives.**

6. Take Decisive Action

Once your plan is clear, make your action powerful and focused. **Drive your action with commitment!** People are drawn to leaders who are committed to something bigger than themselves. When you have done your homework in steps 1–5, you can stand and say, "The train is leaving the station, get on board or be left behind."

7. Feedback Systems

Set up systems to help you monitor progress towards your vision and adjust your plans and actions as necessary. Once committed to, **the vision remains the same.** Don't keep changing the vision, **change the plans and actions!**

The next question I ask is, "Which of these seven steps, if you took the company's mind-set as a whole, is complete?" Most are not even on step one. Many don't even have alignment at the executive team level, and some CEOs have not even given serious thought to describing the vision, mission and values of the company.

I am not asking the executive team to dance around a fire under the full moon, but I do ask them to create a powerful intent through pictures, films, company meetings, PowerPoint presentations and other modern methods to make clear, and build commitment to, the corporation's vision, mission, strategy and values. As our modern hunting tribes become larger and more diverse, compelling visions become more important, not less. Each employee should be committed to a clear picture of the overall vision and mission, and of their part in achieving success.

As an individual, you cannot create what you can't conceive. Like a builder without a blueprint trying to tell his construction crew each day what to build, a leader of an organization will not succeed if he is not able to conceive, communicate, and build commitment to a vision for the future. Energy will be wasted on false starts and journeys that lead to dead ends while wasting time and money.

Key elements to discovering and manifesting vision are:
- Visualizing the opportunity
- Objectively understanding the pros and cons
- Communicating the vision to the team
- Defining the structure that will support the vision
- Being open to adjustments in plans and actions
- Being the defender of the vision

COMMITMENT

"Until one is committed, there is hesitancy, the chance to draw back, always ineffectiveness concerning all acts of initiative and creation."

—Goethe

When I was a leader in a groundbreaking consulting firm, we taught our consultants to tell stories instead of give advice. People resist advice and teaching, but accept stories. Storytelling to pass on wisdom and knowledge preceded the written word. The activity of storytelling automatically connects people to a primal feeling that something important is about to happen.

It was important to our consulting practice that all our leadership consultants had a consistent approach to the work. We were working with global companies who had divisions all over the world. They did not want different corporate cultures to develop in different areas of the company, and they expected a consistent approach by all our consultants. Additionally, as you might imagine, it is hard to create commitment to practices with highly-educated leadership consultants who had their own ideas about what worked. It is said that leading a consulting firm is like herding cats.

Success Stories

To create commitment to our practices, the partners would begin by telling success stories that illustrated our best practices. We would then spend the first day of our four-day quarterly meetings letting our leadership consultants tell their success stories. This was always our consultants favorite day. Like successful hunters around a camp fire, they got to tell stories about their victories, while the younger members of the team learned. Each story would have a beginning describing the problem, a middle explaining how the problem was solved, and an end that talked about the results. We would always comment on how this was an example of our best business practices. Our team knowledge was multiplied, we all felt a feeling of connection, and commitment to our practices was built naturally. Often we would bring in clients to tell their success stories while working with our leadership consultants. We felt that this day was more important to the consultants than their pay.

Likewise, we taught our clients, who were trying to change their organizational culture, or implement a new strategy, to tell stories. We explained that they had to create a mythology of success that was passed on naturally by stories. We helped them construct those stories, and at some point in time, they took on a life of their own.

The technique is simple. Tell a story about a time when you faced a similar strategic problem and succeeded. Ask the team members to do the same. Conduct a dialogue that is focused only on how to solve the problem. Avoid debates. As ideas come up, make notes and assign accountabilities for actions to be followed-up in the next meeting.

Over time, conducting this process creates commitment to the strategy and uncovers the road to the strategy. Your team participates, and both you and the team learn. Commitment around the cognitive roadmap and the visceral feeling are strong, and you are ready to win.

We discovered the truth of the ancient method of creating commitment while working with a client in the UK. Because of visa limitations, we had to rotate our consultants. Over time, all of our one-hundred-plus consultants had to serve time in the UK. The client said to us at the end of the engagement, "When we first started this rotation, we thought we would eventually reach the bottom of the barrel, but we didn't. All your consultants have a consistent quality and approach." They were amazed. We simply explained that we used the same techniques to create our organizational culture that we taught their leaders to use, which reinforced the entire program.

Commitment to Something Beyond Yourself

Our consulting firm was committed to "Making a difference in the lives of people and the performance of organizations." Manifesting this vision became more important than any individual agenda. Even after many of us left the firm, we all are still committed to this vision. I can remember walking into a large ballroom with the founder of the firm after one of our best years. We had invited all consultants and their families to join us in a celebration in Hawaii for a week of meetings and fun. The level of gratitude, energy and celebration was beyond words. The founder and I turned to each other and simultaneously said, "Look what you have created." I will never forget that moment. We created something bigger than ourselves, and it was the greatest feeling. Nothing inspires people, and creates deeper commitment, than working together to create something greater than yourself.

Life Begins With Need and Grows to Commitment

In modern life, children begin their journey totally dependent upon their parents and soon learn to express their needs. We cry as infants, throw fits as children, and manipulate as young adults. Becoming a responsible adult is the process of becoming less selfish and more committed to others. If we are raised with a relatively high level of security, vertical leaps in maturity or selflessness occur at marriage, after having children, and when becoming committed to spiritual or secular communities. The results of these leaps are increased productivity, accountability, compassion, and improved relationships. These leaps are stimulated by becoming committed to something bigger, like the northern plains tribes' commitment to doubling food production to survive the next winter. Becoming committed to something larger can stimulate an expansion of the human spirit. Succeeding generates further expansion.

Experienced leaders create or find "something bigger" that the entire team can be committed to creating—a business strategy, a place of honor in the marketplace, becoming the best, blazing new trails, or creating a place to work that brings results and fulfillment. The leader's commitment creates great energy; as Ralph Lauren, founder of a great 20th century fashion empire said:

"A leader has the vision and conviction that a dream can be achieved. He inspires the power and energy to get it done."

In the modern world, it is not the elements that destroy organizations, it is fierce competition. A business, like the tribe, can cease to exist. People do not starve to death, but their quality of life diminishes and their confidence and spirit contracts.

Commitment and Intention

At some point in time, commitment becomes intentionality. Commitment moves from a sense of need to a clear picture and feeling regarding a future state. From the present, your consciousness can perceive the path to success. Many have written about the power of this kind of commitment fueled with intention. Goethe, a well-known German thinker, said:

"Until one is committed, there is hesitancy, the chance to draw back, always ineffectiveness concerning all acts of initiative and creation. There is one elementary truth, the ignorance of which kills countless ideas and splendid plans; that the moment one definitely commits oneself, then providence moves too, all sorts of things occur to help one that would never otherwise have occurred. A whole stream of events issues from the decision raising in one's favor all manner of unforeseen events, meetings and material assistance which no one could have dreamed would have come their way. Whatever you can do or dream you can, begin it. Boldness has genius, power and magic in it. Begin it now!"

Yet, how many times has someone asked you if you were committed? Too many, one would imagine. You want to give some smart answer like, "not this week" or "funny you should ask, I just gave up commitment." What kinds of feelings arise when someone pushes you to become more committed? Do you feel anxious, trapped, pushed, or abused?

Many people avoid commitment for a number of reasons that we won't go into here. Yet commitment is a powerful tool in life and in business. As a leader, you must learn to create commitment and have the courage to fan its flames into powerful intention.

Look backwards into your own life and see if this is not true. I can count a number of occasions when I was totally committed to something and, in fact, as Goethe said, "All sorts of things occurred to help."

What is it like to be around a committed person? There seems to be a great intensity, an attraction that draws you into whatever they are doing. They seem to shine. No matter how badly things go, they get up and try even harder the next time. They may lose a battle, but they will not lose the war. Sometimes they just drive you crazy, but most times you admire them, even if you don't agree with their point of view.

Even more powerful is a committed team. Have you ever had to face a truly committed team in sports or business? It is very intimidating. They have this look in their eyes and confidence in their voice. I like to watch the interviews prior to a playoff game. Sometimes you can tell which team is truly committed to winning and which team is only saying, "We are going to do our best." The team that wins is always the one that intends to win.

The sense of commitment is not bragging or overshooting with hyperbole; that would be far worse than simply "trying your best or working hard." There is a feeling around a committed person or team that is truly dialed into the objective like an F16 that is locked onto its target. It is calm, focused and powerful: hard to explain, but easy to recognize.

Goethe said, *"Assistance which no one could have dreamed would have come their way."* How is that? Is it luck or what? My grandfather said, "Luck is when preparation meets with opportunity." Certainly, people who are prepared and committed are more likely to see and seize an opportunity. They are always looking for chances at success. A leader who is committed, more often than not, finds a way to succeed. They are relentless, and thus inspire their teams to be the same way. But is there more to this?

The physics department at MIT noticed that an extremely large number of student hypotheses proved to be true after experimentation. Way beyond what would be statistically reasonable. So the administration launched an investigation to search for cheating. They found none, but one of the faculty members started an experiment to determine if the intentions of the students were actually affecting the outcomes.

Electron guns were set up to throw electrons against a surface that had an opening. Three groups had exactly the same setup. The students in group one were told to make observations but given no indication of what they might expect to see. In group two, students were asked not to touch anything, but to imagine electrons passing through the opening. Group three was asked to do the opposite and imagine them hitting the surface of the plate.

One is unable to see electrons with the naked eye. The counts were done electronically. In every case, the electrons responded consistent with the observer's instructions. When the students in group two were instructed to imagine the electrons passing through the opening, they did so much more often than in group one; and the same thing happened in group three which was instructed to imagine them hitting the surface. Could Goethe's observation indicate that the power of commitment and intention actually affects the flow of the physical world?

Certainly commitment and intention affect economic affairs. Many economists feel that the Great Depression was caused by what they call a "Self-Fulfilling Prophecy." Look at the stock market today. At one time, it seemed like stocks could go no higher, but they did, way beyond reason. Then, when the fall was in full swing, it seemed stocks could not go any lower, but they did. Momentum is a known and accepted factor in the financial markets. What more is this than intention or commitment to a belief? That which a group of traders has decided becomes a true, self-fulfilling prophecy.

Clearly, the total available markets for your products and the products of other companies are generally huge. Most markets are far from saturated and many wait to be stimulated by creative leaders. A strongly held belief or commitment by a market leader has often not only stimulated a market, but created new markets.

The question for you to consider is, what are you committed to? Are you and your team totally committed to your business goals, or is there hesitancy?

"... Hesitancy, the chance to draw back, always ineffec- tiveness concerning all acts of initiative and creation..."

When you lead a team you must be the first to commit, and the combined level of commitment, or lack of it, will affect your performance. If each member becomes totally committed to their part on the team, it will surely affect your overall performance. So, I ask the question again, are you committed? Remember:

"Boldness has genius, power and magic in it. Begin it now!"

Creating Commitment

We have talked about the positive and negative effects of commitment. Commitment is a powerful tool to organize and focus your personal, family and organization's efforts. The boldness of commitment, as Goethe said, *"... has genius, power and magic in it."* But how do leaders create commitment in the hearts and minds of their teams?

Demanding commitment is not the answer. You can shout and scream, "You have to be committed, there is no room in this organization for those who are not com- mitted," but that will create a team full of fear and resistance, and more likely resistance than fear. People may be afraid to say they are not committed in front of you, but they will talk and laugh about you and the ridiculous demands that you make. They may work long hours, but the guiding belief behind their work will be to prove that what you say is impossible. They may think you are crazy to believe such impossible and foolish dreams when, in fact, the commitment you insist on is entirely possible if people knew what you knew.

Having your team know what you know is certainly the first step in creating commitment. There are two aspects to sharing what you know. One is a content-based roadmap that you have constructed in your mind based on your past experiences, and your ability to project those experiences into a picture of a future possibility. The second is the visceral feeling of confidence and possibility you project.

Both are important, but you cannot do one without the other. You can't tell the story of your strategy if you don't truly believe it to be possible. People will easily see through your words. There will be a hollowness and lack of congruency between your words and feelings. In other words, you cannot "fake it." Therefore, if you are asked to create commitment to a strategy you do not believe in, you need to work with the team or leader who is asking you to sell that commitment until you truly believe in it.

Once you truly believe in the possibility, it is time to start selling. Yes, selling, not commanding. Remember, you need to have your team truly believe through a cognitive roadmap and a visceral feeling. Also, keep in mind that your team may not have the extensive experiential background that you bring to the table. They do not have your exact experiences or knowledge. Your job is to find out what experiences and knowledge they have and transfer enough of yours, so they can see the road to the future, and feel confident in getting there. Then you can combine your understanding with theirs. Oftentimes, the combination of knowledge and understanding by you and your team will create a wisdom that is greater than the sum of the parts. With success, you now have a team of people committed to taking your strategy from words on paper to economic reality.

Telling People What to Do?

If you cannot get your team to this point, you will have to direct their every activity. If your team is loyal to you, or afraid of you, they will follow orders. In this way, if you have a clear picture of the roadmap in your head, you can have them do the things that will lead to your strategy without full commitment on their part. Many leaders use this strategy with some success, but it has at least three fatal flaws.

First, it is hard to achieve scale. You can direct the activities of a small organization but, as that organization grows, you lose bandwidth and misdirection or hesitancy occurs. People either wait for their orders or innocently go off in the wrong direction. In either case, time and money is wasted, which affects time to market, market share, pricing and profit margins. It is always more effective to have a clear understanding engrained in the consciousness of your team as the directional force, and it will save you time as a leader. With the time, you can work on new strategic directions.

Second, your team has little ownership. There is no real feeling of being a part of something that is important. No visceral energy, just a job, stock options and a paycheck. Without the energy that comes from creating something you are committed to, "burn-out" occurs sooner, rather than later. The people have a short-term perspective instead of a long-term commitment, and the grass always looks greener on the other side. Hence, people leave for what they see as a better opportunity. The result is increased attrition instead of increased effort during hard times.

Third, creativity suffers. There are many roads to the future. Shortcuts and methods to increase speed exist and can be taken advantage of if people have a clear picture of the destination. When you are holding the destination in your head and giving out turns along the road, there is no possibility for "Relentless Improvement." In fact, improvement is constrained by a factor of one: your understanding of the road to success. You lose the wisdom and power of the team when you lead in a totally directive fashion.

Find the Wisdom of the Team

How, then, do you combine your understanding with your team's to create commitment? Knowing they don't know all that you know, and may not be able to conceive of possibilities beyond their experience, you need to begin by finding out what they know, what limitations they believe in, and how they truly feel about your strategy.

Once you have achieved this, then you can work on filling in the gaps or creating synergy that reaches beyond the sum of the parts.

The first step is creating trust. If people don't feel safe in sharing their insights and understandings, the dialogue you have may be focused on them trying to please you. If you consider their ideas to be wrong, and are trying to manipulate them to your point of view, you might as well just tell them and be directive. At least that is honest. You have to create a safe environment for exploration. Listen to your team before you share your ideas, and spend time developing mutual understanding, not debating. Then, as you talk, you will uncover what they really see and feel.

Finding Common Ground

Finding out what the team knows, and what aligns with your picture, is the second step. This is what we call finding common ground. People find it easier to disagree than to agree. Any organization will always have its areas of conflict at the top of mind before its areas of harmony. It is human nature. Arguments and debates start and spread easily and are hard to stop. So, as a leader, you must be relentless in first finding common ground. What are the things we agree on in terms of goals and methods for getting there? Once you have achieved the situation in which you know what they know, and they know what you know, you share common ground around a number of issues. This important first step creates a good feeling of fellowship and mutual commitment, and a platform from which to solve problems.

Storytelling

In the third step, if the strategies you want to create commitment around are aggressive, there is a high likelihood that your team will not see the road to them. They will have developed what we call limiting beliefs around various actions that lead to your strategy.

How do you move people beyond these beliefs? As I pointed out earlier, storytelling is very effective. Don't forget to tell stories that create commitment to your vision, mission and business strategy.

Become the Guardian of the Vision

Once this purpose is established, the leader must hold the vision or mission high. While being continuously open to input during creation, the leader should become the guardian once the vision or mission is established. This purpose will become the template for all activities, both strategic and tactical. The manifestation should be seen as central to the success of the enterprise and all who gain a livelihood from its growth. All team members must feel that achieving this purpose transcends their personal agendas. The leader must be prepared to take a strong stand against those who would tear down the team's purpose.

Key elements to creating commitment are:

- Remember that commitment releases energy
- Find something worthy of commitment
- Deepening commitment beyond business goals
- Spreading commitment to all members of the team
- Using commitment to create during the journey
- Integrating intention with commitment

CREATING INSIGHT

1. The ability to see and understand clearly the **inner nature** *of things, esp. by intuition.*

2. A clear understanding of the **inner nature** *of some specific thing.*

—Webster's New World Dictionary

If you compared all of human knowledge with the unknown, human knowledge would be dwarfed by the vastness of what remains undiscovered. It seems the more you learn, the more you realize how much mystery remains. This realization itself creates curiosity and a vertical leap in understanding.

Albert Einstein once said:

"I did not create or invent, I merely discovered realities that were previously unknown."

It is Already There

While working with one of my clients, Sylmark, which does direct marketing through infomercials, I met Steve Ober, SVP and Partner. Steve directs and produces most of their shows. His success record is far greater than anyone in the industry. Seven out of ten of his shows produce successful levels of sales. The industry average is one to two out of twenty. So I asked him why he was so successful. He said,

"I am driven to win and the answers are already there. If you work hard enough, you will find them."

He also said,

"I know what I want, because I can see it."

He went on to explain he never gives up until the show is exactly right. He said that he stays humble, and always looks for a better way before releasing his shows.

After listening to his story, I told him about a movie Martin Scorsese recently produced about the life and career of Bob Dylan. As the story is told, they cut to an interview conducted with Bob Dylan recently. Bob Dylan comments on the various stages in his life. In his commentary, it became obvious to me that Dylan understood what Einstein was talking about and many CEOs struggle to understand. Dylan discovered the needs and wants of his market and became the voice of his generation, while transforming American folk music from the backrooms of Greenwich Village to a global craze.

In response to people saying he was the voice of a generation, he commented that, "It was already there." He explained throughout the movie that he noticed how people would respond positively to various aspects of singers like Woody Guthrie, Pete Seeger and many others. Each singer had certain things that would connect with the audience: the look in their eyes, the tone of voice, the way they picked the strings on their guitar and combined great singing with meaningful words. What the generation wanted was already out there but not embodied in one person.

Dylan observed and then let go of the aspects of his act that were not connecting, and adopted all of the elements that were connecting with the audiences. He literally became the voice of a generation by discovering existing realities and combining his intention and creativity with the needs he noticed in his audience. It seemed simple to him. He could see the future success by observing what was happening in the moment. He truly unleashed his genius by living Integrative Presence and connecting with an existing intelligence.

When he returned to Minnesota after only five months in New York City, which was the center of folk music at the time, he had been transformed from an okay singer to a genius. Many from Minnesota commented on what seemed to be a magical transformation. One said, "It was almost like he had sold his soul to the Devil." But, of course, he didn't, he simply developed, as it says in Webster's, "A clear understanding of the inner nature of some specific thing." Through a series of insights, he discovered an existing reality, combined it with his genius, and became the voice of a generation.

To make that transition Dylan, had to let go of his past and be in the moment. He even changed his last name, and often says that it really does not matter who he was in the past. This is the first step that leads to insight and discovery.

After listening to the story, Steve Ober said, "Exactly, and that just shows what a great film maker Martin Scorsese is."

Steve Ober and Dylan have mastered insight and have formed the habit of discovering "A clear understanding of the **inner nature** of some specific thing." There genius is truly unleashed.

Columbus did not create the "New World," he merely discovered a place that Europeans didn't know existed. However, he had to first leave the safety of the shore and venture out into the unknown. A requirement for improved levels of understanding is letting go of what you think you know. He had examined theories that the world was round, not flat, but most of all, he looked out at the horizon and could see the curvature. He could see ships disappear below the horizon as they went out to sea. He examined the evidence, but somehow he just knew.

Most people get locked into what they know, and thereby lock out possibility and discovery. When leaders do this, they become stale and cliché. Like a television rerun played for the fourteenth time, they can't hold the interest of their people.

Always a Better Way

Leaders are the first to discover the existence of realities that are critical to the success of their companies. They continuously seek a deeper understanding of themselves, the market place, their teams, and the world in general. They look beyond the shadow into substance.

If a leader wants to discover new realities, that leader has to find ways to expand the consciousness, thought and behaviors of an organization; then it follows that a leader must become master of creating insight. The best leaders that I have worked with have created insight at every level: on PowerPoint slides, in presentations, in a conversation, at staff meetings, all employee meetings, addressing the market, and on TV interviews. Without new insights, new records in earnings, profits and market share cannot be created.

Insight enables you to conceive possibilities never experienced. In some mysterious way, it synthesizes your existing knowledge, adds a form of innate wisdom and reveals possibilities that were not previously understood. It happens in an instant. It is an "AHA!" Suddenly things that seemed unclear seem clear. After insight, what you see seems obvious, even though it was invisible to you moments ago.

In this chapter, we will examine why it is so difficult to create insight and how to succeed in creating that insight. Business is like a team sport, and sports can form a microcosmic laboratory to help us understand the key elements of success in this regard.

New records are set in sports and new realities in business are created year after year, because insight enables you to conceive possibilities never experienced. All those who have left a trail of greatness take time to create insight. The most effective business leaders, while they are pleased with their success, seek a better way. After becoming the leader of the most profitable corporation in the world, Jack Welch spent most of his year-end speech on General Electric's trying to create insight about even greater possibilities for next year.

When the accepted limits of performance are broken, improvements and discoveries spread at increased rates. As discussed before, at one time no one believed a man could run the mile in less than four minutes and now you have to do it to make a high school track team.

The First Experience

One way philosophers have divided human experience is into the realms of "Pure Experience," and "Concepts," including beliefs, judgments, comparisons and duality. They have also defined the first human experience as birth, and how this first experience of the world colors our judgment of reality.

Imagine you are in the womb. You're surrounded by warm fluids, you have "room service" so you don't have to search for food, the light is muted and sounds are soft. More important, you are safe within the person who loves you. You are immersed in unconditional love.

Suddenly, the fluid disappears; you feel pressure from all sides and are then forced through a small passage. You're exposed to bright light, cold air, and you might even be spanked. Your life support system is cut off; you're stuck with pins and temporarily taken from your mother. What might you conclude from this experience?

Some psychologists believe that even though a newborn doesn't have a belief system yet, a deep association is created between change and pain. Later in life, around the age of two, you start pulling stuff off tables and are told you are bad, or even worse, you are hit. You begin to develop a survival pattern that reduces pain. This pattern becomes encoded in your psyche and drives much of your life experience to come.

Right/wrong, win/lose, beginning/end—these patterns form what psychologists call a "Belief System" or "World View." This world view forms a "window of perception" that then filters our experience, so we rarely experience true reality; we mostly see reality through beliefs and judgments.

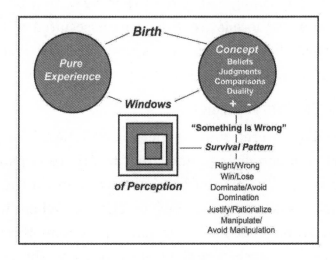

When an anorexic person looks in a mirror, they see a person who's fat. That's not reality, but that's how their belief system colors their reality. That is an extreme example, but we all filter reality to fit into our belief systems. Racial prejudice is another example. If you believe, or have been told by someone you respect, that certain races are bad, you will filter reality and lock in on the parts of reality that reinforce your belief system. Wars and other atrocities have been created by this problem. The main factor driving this phenomenon is the need to be right about our existing perceptions and beliefs.

How will this limit your success and growth? By filtering reality based on decisions we have made in the past, we are missing large parts of reality that may be relevant to our decision making process. If we are prisoners of our beliefs, which experiences will we be most locked into and hardest us to change? It is the experiences that proved us right, because there is great pleasure associated with those experiences. The danger here is that what has worked in the past may not work now.

Change Leads to Expansion

If you've discovered that a belief you once held is no longer correct, you can change and grow, but there is pain with that growth. The pain of being wrong is one of the major reasons we are so resistant to change. When we feel uncomfortable, defensive, or pained by something, this could be our psyche's way of alerting us to the need for growth and expansion of our window of perception. Unfortunately, we don't tend to jump for joy and enthusiastically take advantage of this opportunity to grow—we tend to get defensive, rationalize and justify our beliefs, rather than search for insight. We do not tend to learn from history or what is happening in the moment. Imagine Bob Dylan's career if he had not changed his style after spending time in New York City.

Since we perceive through the window of perception formed by our belief system, each of us can only perceive parts of reality. Some people experience bigger parts of reality in certain situations than others do. What's worse, we tend to want to be right about our existing beliefs because they have led us to our present levels of success. The result is, when we approach an experience, we select the parts that fit our belief system. This is called "selective perception" (remember the Old Lady/Young Lady). We go into an experience with "Belief System A" and leave that experience with the same belief system. This creates a survival pattern around particular experiences.

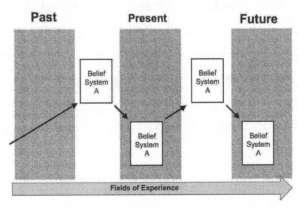

Gaining New Insight

It's important to note that all beliefs that drive our behavior are not necessarily conscious. Many beliefs are totally unconscious. These subconscious beliefs are often in conflict with our conscious beliefs. A person may consciously believe in success, but due to a subconscious belief such as, "I don't have the right background, and I am not as smart as people think," that person will find himself doing things to limit his success.

Organizations are a collection of conscious and unconscious belief systems, and often the conscious or stated beliefs are in conflict with the unstated beliefs. This is why a corporation can have a goal of increasing revenue by 20%, while most people in the corporation do not really believe the goal will be achieved.

If we are locked into our belief systems, and are selecting realities that match our belief systems because we need to be right, is there any hope for change? Once a behavior pattern is established, it tends to be repeated unless interrupted by a consequence or experience powerful enough to challenge the beliefs and assumptions that drive such behavior. If indeed the experience is strong enough that it drives us to insight and reflection, we might form a new belief or assumption, which in turn changes our behaviors and actions. So does all change only come through pain? Or might we be able to see through others' "windows of perception" and learn a new way?

When we approach a field of experience that challenges us or is bigger than our belief system, we experience discomfort in a number of ways: anger, fear, depression, gloom or irritation. To deal with these feelings, we have basically two choices: rationalization or reflection.

Rationalization finds ways to accept the challenge to our perception through blaming, feigning ignorance, making excuses or hoping things will change to suit our belief system. We search to find confirmation of our belief systems and rationalization is our main tool. A complication is that many people feel they will benefit from agreeing with and supporting their leader's belief system.

Our other choice, reflection, provides an opportunity for growth. When you are challenged by an experience and feel uncomfortable or fearful, stop and reflect. Try challenging your existing perception. This is difficult because you're going to have to admit in some way that your prior belief system was wrong. Humans hate to be wrong, but those who are consistently successful have created a habit of reflection. After deep reflection you can leave an experience with a belief system that's

expanded. You don't totally discard "Belief System A"—
you come out of reflection with "Belief System A + B".

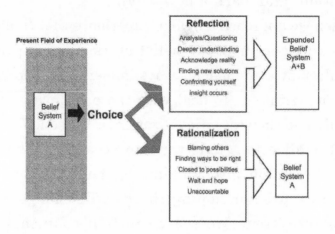

The larger belief system is more effective because you
perceive a bigger part of reality, just as Dylan did as he
was observing the aspects of other singers that appealed to
audiences. You see more of the business situation and are
able to make more effective decisions. Confronting your
belief systems is painful, but after you have integrated a
new insight into your belief system, you feel great, excited,
inspired. Your level of aliveness goes up dramatically.

This wider window of perception produces increased
vision. Vision is not just into "the big picture," but also into
all aspects of your life. Leaders with larger windows of
perception have the vision to see the pathways to success
in ever-changing marketplaces, the vision to see the
solutions to daily problems and the vision to communicate
in a way that their team can hear. Vision, and the ability

to communicate that vision in a compelling manner that creates insight, are the two factors that distinguish great leaders. Teams with great leaders are always more successful than those without.

Insight creates expanded windows of perception. If your windows of perception or belief systems are expanding, what might you experience?

1. Deeper levels of insight and vision into future business trends
2. Clearer understanding of your team members
3. The excitement of discovering a bigger piece of reality
4. Stronger relationships with friends and family, deeper insight into others
5. A feeling of peace that comes from reflection
6. Better corporate performance as you learn to develop others
7. Better understanding of competitors
8. Better understanding of customers and their needs
9. Less anger and frustration and more understanding and wisdom

Seeing Through Your Team's Windows

Business is like a team sport, just more complicated. Championships are won by teams of people who take ownership of a common vision, who are open to possibility, who trust each other, are persistent, proactive and relentlessly seek personal and professional improvement. Winning teams need leaders with vision. The greatest leaders consistently discover and manifest visions that create strategic advantage, enliven the human spirit, and create business performance.

If you feel that teamwork is not necessary to run an organization, then you should stop reading at this point. The principles that follow will help you draw out the genius in individuals and synchronize those individuals into high performance teams.

Change Leader's Discovery

When I was working as a change leader for a large conglomerate in the 70's, I was assigned a manufacturing plant that was last in the division. This was my first assignment in this industry and the plant manager had hired me not realizing I had no experience in this industry. After moving my family to this remote location, I was giving the division manager a tour through the plant while peppering him with questions about how the machinery worked. Suddenly he stopped and asked, "Paul, you don't seem to know much about our industry." I explained that I had not previously worked in this industry, but had a knack for solving problems. He explained that I had better learn quickly because it was very technical.

To speed up my learning, I decided to spend a lot of time on the midnight shift asking questions. No one listens to people on the midnight shift, so I thought I could not do myself much damage. While standing next to a machine, I asked the operator how the production level could be improved. He explained to me that it was easy, but no one listened to him.

I promised that I would listen, and somehow he believed me. It was a machine that picked up rough parts, moved them to a spot on the machine, worked that part, and then moved it to another part of the machine until the work was done. Over the years the parts had gotten smaller, but no one thought to reduce the length of the armature that moved the part. Reducing the length would speed up transfer and nearly double the productivity.

He still insisted that no one would do anything about this and that he was just wasting his breath. I said that I would call in the maintenance man and rig the machine if he would help. He relished the idea of getting the maintenance man out of bed so agreed. I had to tell the maintenance man that it was an emergency and when he arrived he was not happy. I told him that doubling productivity was in fact an emergency, and he decided to help.

We got that machine running that night and it did in fact double productivity. I could not pay the machine operator a bonus because he was in the union, but I gave him overtime to train others and oversee the conversion of the other 16 machines. We named the production standard after him, and from that point on, people came to me with ideas. I asked questions, synthesized peoples' ideas, and we became the number one plant in the division.

The fact that I knew almost nothing about the industry, and had no preconceived thoughts about how things should be, unleashed my genius. I had to explore and uncover the genius within all the employees to succeed. From that moment on, I learned to ask questions with the intent of uncovering hidden understandings and genius. I still use the same approach today as I work with executives of Fortune 500 companies and mid-sized companies. People know more than they realize, and if you can connect with them, see their genius, and draw it out, great things can be accomplished.

Listen to Your Team

If you are a strong leader, when you hold a strong view on a subject, do those who follow you tend to agree or disagree? Most of the time, the team will agree with you. Some may disagree, but most often there is general agreement. How might this limit your success? The team might see possibilities that are outside your window of perception and not be willing to tell you what they see.

When we are leaders, we have two forces working against us: One, we only see what our belief system or window of perception allows us to see. Two, often our team wants to please us and finds ways to agree with what we see, instead of giving us the benefit of what they see through their unique window of perception. Often, even when our team members give us what they really see, we make them wrong and close down their input, because we can't see through their window of perception.

A team will perceive a larger portion of reality than one person can. There will be overlap (hopefully not too much) and there will be team members out in left field, but the team's overall perception of reality will be greater than any single leader's. Unfortunately, most of us never learn to hear what the members of our team are saying. Most leaders do not realize they are doing this, but when we talk to their teams confidentially, they tell us:

1. Mistakes are made that could have been avoided
2. Opportunities are missed
3. The leader appears less than effective to the team
4. The team feels resentment about not being listened to
5. The team starts to clam-up: "He/She doesn't listen anyway"
6. The leader starts blaming the team for mistakes they warned him/her about
7. Distance grows between the leader and the team
8. The leader becomes isolated and his understanding of the business shrinks
9. The leader loses the respect of the team
10. Corporate performance drops
11. The leader is replaced with someone who has a bigger window of perception

We are not suggesting that a leader should give up his decision-making role or create committees that never reach a conclusion. We are suggesting that a leader learn how to tap the wisdom of the team to create insight before making decisions.

Reflection is one way to break this pattern of not seeing through others' windows, and coaching is the other. To break any behavioral pattern, a leader must get help from an objective source. Since most members of that leader's team would find it hard to be objective, an outsider is often effective in helping break the pattern and then developing the habit of reflection. The purpose of the off-sites I have conducted over the years is to help leaders break the patterns that limit their perception, and to teach them to lead an organization that uses all of its potential and perceptive abilities.

This is what it looks like when a leader is open to the views of others:

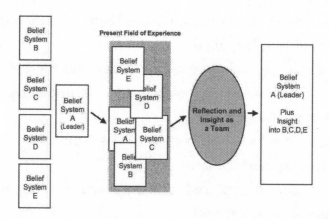

It is easier to see through others' windows of perception than it is to open your own. You gain the advantage of an expanded belief system without going through the pain of opening your own window of perception. Combining both the opening of your own window and seeing through your team's window, can be powerful. In seeing what your team sees, you may even experience insight yourself, as I did.

Continuous Performance Improvement

Great athletes and teams know that there is always room for improvement. New records are set year after year. Sages say they know nothing because they are aware that the unknown is so much greater than the known. All those who have left a trail of greatness are busy looking forward to their next discovery, because discovery is a reward unto itself.

Certain experiences seem to accelerate discovery. When the accepted limits of performance are broken, improvements and discoveries spread faster. As I said earlier, at one time no one believed a man could run the mile in less than four minutes, fly faster than the speed of sound or walk on the moon. Breaking these barriers created new realities and accelerated performance in running, aviation and technology.

Our experience tells us that there are natural extensions of events that lead to performance breakthroughs. One insight stimulates an even greater insight. Small breakthroughs come first and build upon each other creating a chain reaction. Unimaginable potentials and energies are released, and people are empowered to make the next discovery.

Targeting Your Team

The most common fault of a business team is that they often focus on defeating the strongest competitors instead of the weakest. I have worked with teams to help them find the fastest and most cost effective route to profitable revenue. I have helped them understand how to identify the strategic window of opportunity where their strengths meet with competitors' weaknesses and the wants of customers. I helped them to clearly describe this window during the consulting process, which becomes part of their value proposition. The following illustrates:

Take the Easy Wins First

Wal-Mart built their retail empire by first developing a superior value proposition by observing, as Dylan did, what aspects of their competitors worked and combined them all into one store, and then built their stores across the street from the weakest competitors, not K-Mart. The traffic was already there, and when people found that the Wal-Mart store embodied everything they wanted, they stopped going to the store across the street. Once they developed strong cash flow and market presence, they began to work on K-Mart, and now, of course, K-Mart's days are numbered.

Had they started by competing with K-Mart early in their development, they would have been defeated or at least slowed considerably. It is my impression that most teams remain task focused on the things they have been doing, instead of observing what is working in a market, and then reinventing themselves. Wal-Mart's competitors did not catch on until it was too late.

Most business organizations have strong beliefs about what seem to be impossible barriers: reducing costs again, increasing profits even more, or taking market share from a dominant competitor. That's because it's hard to conceive of performance levels never experienced, or find events that open people to the possibility of dramatic performance improvements. The goal is to use experience and insight to guide leaders, and all employees, to the performance breakthroughs that will start a chain reaction of accelerated performance. A leader's goal is to bring their team to the point where relentless improvement becomes part of the fabric and passion of everyday life.

Creating Original Thought

When I was working with a large phone company, a regulatory change was dominating the conversations at every level. The State had changed the requirement for returning lines to service from 24 hours to 4 hours. This seemed like the last straw in a chain of "regulatory interferences." I was leading them through a session to help them deal with this problem.

To comply with this new regulation, the phone company would have to buy new trucks and hire crews to have the coverage needed to comply. Most felt that there was no amount of trucks that would really meet the requirement. All people could think about was how stupid the regulators were. People were literally fuming.

I asked the team if they would be willing to try a process that was a little outside the norm in hopes that we might find a solution to this problem. They agreed out of desperation. I explained that if this process was to work at all, they would have to follow instructions exactly. They agreed.

I had them sit in a circle with no tables or note pads and explained the following.

I said that the purpose of this exercise was to create original thought that would lead to a solution to the problem we discussed. I also pointed out that once the team experienced original thought, everyone would instantly recognize the truth of those thoughts and would not likely ever forget. I promised, however, that once we reached this level of understanding, I would capture that thought on the flip chart. Therefore, no notes would be needed.

I explained that there are three kinds of thought. The first is the type of thought that comes out of people over and over again. It is a phrase that has been said many times and you can almost see it coming before it is spoken. I said we call this, "Old Wine," sometimes spelled "Whine." Everyone laughed nervously as I said we will have none of this.

The second kind of thought is what is called "good ideas." Consultants are famous for collecting these ideas on flip charts, having them typed and sending them to their clients to sort out. Most often no one does anything with these ideas. Good ideas are often "old wine" in disguise. I explained that we will have none of these, and assigned the leader the job of helping me identify these when they occurred.

What we are looking for is "original thought." In order to reach original thought you have to let go of all thoughts you have previously had about this topic. You have to be willing to explore the unknown. You must be willing to be wrong and entertain partially complete thoughts. As a matter of fact, in the beginning of this process, I only wanted partially complete thoughts.

I went on to say that to get ready for this exercise, you will have to understand how to truly listen to the other members of the team. The team wisdom can create original thought if everyone listens to each other. I explained that you cannot listen while you are processing your own thoughts.

I drew this graphic on the flip chart and asked the team what kind of thoughts they have while others are speaking. The following were typical:

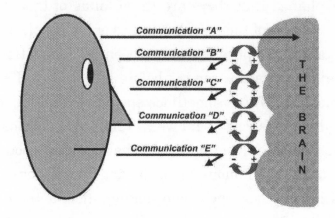

- Is what this person saying right or wrong?
- What response can I give?
- What is my idea and how should I state it?
- How can I look good during this?

I explained that great listeners intake first and then process information, just as speed readers do not think about what they are reading as they read. They just intake and the brain remembers everything. After all, if you are thinking while you are doing intake, nothing gets recorded in your memory banks and, of course, you cannot recall. I explained that I would give people time to process, but asked people not to process while others were talking. You could almost smell wires burning.

I explained that the process would be as follows:

1. We would frame the problem
2. A person who feels inspired would say what was coming to them ... not a complete thought
3. Between each persons sharing, there would be a three second pause to process thoughts, and I would keep time
4. Then the next person would share, not trying to spring board off the other, but just share what comes up
5. We will follow this process until the team has an insight which is likely to be an original thought

I explained that when the original thought appeared, we would all recognize it, and we would stop and capture that thought; until then, no note-taking.

At first this was painful and we had to call "Old Whine" and "Good Ideas" a couple of times, but finally the team got into a rhythm. People started to feel comfortable sharing ideas that came to them, and the ideas began to fit together until a huge insight came.

They discovered a technical solution that would create a back-up system on all lines that would automatically connect should there be a break of any kind in the first line. It would be an investment, but nothing like hundreds of trucks and crews. This afternoon saved over a billion dollars.

What happened was the group achieved "Integrative Presence" together and connected themselves with "The

Great Intelligence." Insight came in the form of thoughts that were totally original. This is a difficult process to facilitate, but a great example of what can be done once a team has the discipline to use these universal principles.

The Nature of Thought

There are many different types of thought, some trap you in circular thinking and others help you dance with the flow of cause and effect. We have explored the route to original thought.

Old Thought: Beliefs, assumptions, and cognitive frameworks stored in the mind during past experiences, which are at best an approximation of reality, and at worst, a distortion.

Comparative Thought: Rethinking of old thoughts to create new frameworks, which are more complex, but still are a rearrangement of old thoughts, often ending in circular thought.

Flowing Thought: Flows during peak experiences, such as being in "The Zone," which is much closer to the nature of reality.

Intention: A state of being that integrates with flowing thought, which influences, in many ways, the flow of cause and effect. I call this combination of flowing thought and intention, **"Integrative Presence."**

Original Thought: Describes the insights experienced during "Integrative Presence." Compared with "old thought" or "comparative thought," these thoughts are genius.

Insight is required for relentless improvement. Breakthroughs in performance come from insight and tend to start chain reactions of accelerated performance and oceans of creativity. Bob Dylan took folk music from a side show to main stream, Wal-Mart went from a discount store to the largest company in the world, and the phone company created a solution that saved billions. All were born from insight into the true nature of things that were there, but no one had discovered.

The key elements to creating insight:
- Never ask questions you think you know the answer to
- After listening, reflect before responding
- Do not process while listening
- Trust the question that comes up from intuition
- "Integrative Presence" creates original thought
- Show humility and curiosity as you ask questions
- Be willing to be wrong even if you think you are right
- Ask questions until mutual insight occurs

STILLNESS AND INTEGRATIVE PRESENCE

"When you lose touch with inner stillness, you lose touch with yourself. When you lose touch with yourself, you lose yourself in the world."

—*Eckhart Tolle, Stillness Speaks*

At the vortex of hurricanes, that raise the sea and blow weak structures from the shore, is stillness. As the stillness at the center of a great hurricane increases, so does its power. Buildings and boats not anchored well are washed away by waves of cyclonic energy. The same is true for great leaders. There is great stillness at their center, and the waves of wisdom that circle them uproot shallow ideas and concepts. Like the hurricane, they are both attractive and frightening. Their stillness generates great power, calm, and insight in the chaos of enterprise.

History is made of many parts, but two are obvious. What actually happened, and our individual or collective perception of what happened. Most people navigate through the world using their perception of what happened in the past to guide the actions of the present and forecast the future. This practice has various levels of success.

The closer a person's perception of reality is to the actual historical reality, the more likely they are to stay on course towards incremental gains. The uphill slope of that course is more certain if that person has been honest with themselves and learned lessons from their mistakes. But no matter how deep the lessons, a person only has that part of history which they perceived, leaving the greater part of reality unconsidered. Growth based on perceived history can only be incremental.

Great leaders often have to make quantum leaps in order to lead their organizations to a vortex of history that is far ahead of most. In fact most great leaders create the future, or at least the future position of their company, in the market place. Great CEOs stimulate the market and create leadership positions, often creating demand that was previously nonexistent. You cannot create a new future by following a road map that is an extension of the past. As Eckhart Tolle says:

"True intelligence operates silently. Stillness is where creativity and solutions to problems are found."

You must be in that place of stillness to observe trends and envision a future state. If you are lost in the world, which is generally attached to historic trends or beliefs formed from the past, your view of the future will be limited. History is essentially a chronicle of thoughts that are all highly filtered. It only provides a general description of what happened. It is often manipulated to fit the views of the historian. A leader can start discovery by understanding history, but that discovery must be completed by a view of present reality that only comes from the stillness of the moment. Like the athlete in the zone, a leader must learn from history, but master letting go to create new realities.

Great leaders master the art of being in the present moment. The most successful know this to be true. The stillness that surrounds the present moment is the cradle for insight. Once you master being in the present, you can envision possibilities, all of which extend themselves only from stillness.

Great Ideas

We have not yet invented time machines. We cannot travel to the past and observe what happened nor can we travel to the future to prepare ourselves. Therefore, we only live in the present moment. There is no reality outside the present moment. The reason we are drawn away from the present is due to comparative thought; the mind wanders into the past and the future. The past only lives in our memory and in writings, all of which are highly filtered by personal views. The future is, at best, a speculation. While learning from the past and having the ability to envision the future are important, the biggest part of reality is in the present. In fact, all reality, other than our thoughts, exists only in the present.

If you depend on comparative thought, you will surely become lost in the limits that are inherent in this kind of thought. Great ideas like: the world is round, Edison's light bulb, or the iPod, come from insight. Business leaders look for ways to access states of mind that produce these kinds of ideas. So over the years I have asked, "When do you get your best ideas?"

People respond with the following:
- In the shower
- When I wake up in the middle of the night
- Early in the morning
- Jogging
- Walking in the forest
- When I least expect it
- While taking a nap
- Swimming
- On vacation

When we discuss the nature of these moments, we find that for one reason or another the mind is still. The circular thoughts that often dominate our mind slow or stop and suddenly the space is opened for insight to occur. We see into the true nature of things because we let go of thoughts that are just a shadow of reality. These thoughts cloud our minds and prevent us from seeing reality. When they circle too fast, they actually narrow our consciousness.

For centuries the best leaders have been able to clear their minds of comparative thought and focus with clarity on the moment. Chuang Tzu (369-269 B.C.) points this out: *"To a mind that is still, the whole universe surrenders."*

Many professional baseball players claim they can see the ball spinning and turning as it approaches at 90 mph. They are able to block out the crowd noise and, mostly, their thoughts. If they were thinking about the last time at bat when they struck out, in that moment, as their mind considers the unfortunate event from the past, the ball flies past and the umpire calls out "strike." On the other hand, should they start to imagine how the crowd will cheer when they hit a home run, as their focus moves from the ball to this fantasy, the ball speeds past. Baseball coaches for years have taught players from the little leagues to the pros to "keep your eye on the ball." One must stay focused to anticipate the future path of the ball and can only connect a round ball with a round bat if they stay focused and in the moment.

A leader who is mentally present can recognize patterns in the moment that lead to the future. One cannot visualize the future without living in the present. The statistics and analysis that businesses often depend on is not enough. That would be like the professional hitter trying to figure out what kind of pitch is coming without watching the ball. Imagine if the only skill a hitter had was to do statistical analysis of the pitcher. The astute player determined that 80% of the time the first pitch was a curve and that there was a pattern of different pitches over the course of an "at bat." This information might help the batter prepare, but it will not substitute for being present and keeping his eye on the ball. As a matter of fact, if the batter is thinking about his research as the ball approaches at 90+ miles per hour, he will definitely be distracted.

Due to cause and effect, the best view of the future is truly seeing how the flow of events is unfolding in the present. A business plan or strategy that does not start with a clear view of the present reality will create a road map that will fail, because the starting point is wrong.

A leader's portal to the future is only through the present. The view through this portal is the only way to stimulate creation that is profound and provides strategic advantage. The great leaders create the future state in their minds based on a realistic view of the present, and then govern their actions based on their aspirations for the future rather, than being "in effect" of the past. Like the baseball hitter in the moment, they can see the trajectory of the future and prepare their organization to take advantage of that trajectory. This is as true for moment to moment decisions as it is for grand strategies.

Personal Presence

A leader whose reality is dominated by thoughts of the past or the future does not appear present. Their personal power is greatly diminished. A leader who is focused on the moment feels powerful and attractive. While working with the Law Department at New York Life, I met some men who worked on John F. Kennedy's staff. I asked them if it was true that you could sense his presence when he entered a room. They said, "Yes"...and that he was present moment to moment when he was campaigning. So much so, that when he met people, even just for a handshake, people felt connected to him. They explained, "He was a master at being in the moment." James Allen (1864-1912) talked about the power of a person in the present when he said:

> *"The strong, calm person is always loved and revered. He is like a shade-giving tree in a thirsty land, or a sheltering rock in a storm."*

True clarity and personal power only exists in the present moment. The question is, how do you do this?

Staying in the Moment

Monks learn to meditate by sitting quietly and then learn to do a walking meditation so that they can carry the stillness they achieved into the world. How can business leaders master this ability? Later in the chapter, we will illustrate a form of meditation that anyone can practice. This process has helped many leaders find peace in the storm of commerce.

As we discussed earlier, having a high level of engagement in life, which includes being connected with "The Great Intelligence," and a low level of attachment, is the first step. The leader who can master this state of mind will stay in the moment more often. This is true mastery.

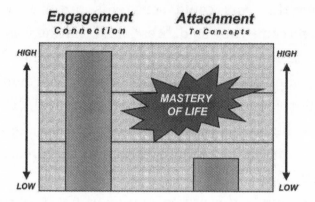

Desert Journey

A friend of mine said to me, "Have you ever spent time alone in the desert?" I replied, "No," and asked why do you ask? He explained to me that I would find this experience transformational and dared me to try. Of course, I could not resist.

He and his wife gave us full instructions and stayed close enough to come to our aid should we need help, but far enough away to be completely out of contact. My wife and I went to separate areas of the desert and set up our individual camps. We were only allowed water, some food and a sleeping bag. No books or reading materials were allowed. We were not allowed to hike around; we had to stay close to our campsite.

They suggested we meditate in the morning and at sunset for twenty minutes facing each of the four directions. They suggested we take a journal to capture our insights. The first day my mind became very active. I packed and repacked by backpack many times. I found new ways to organize the campsite. I found a snake bite kit and read the instructions over and over again trying to distract myself. Finally, I ran out of things to do, and began to sit quietly and meditate as suggested, facing the four directions. Then I decided that since it was dark, and I had nothing to do or read, that I would crawl into my sleeping bag and sleep through the night.

I was not asleep for long when a pack of coyotes running through the valley woke me. I was sleeping on my back and as I opened my eyes I could see the stars. Because of the lack of humidity in the desert, they were sharper than I had ever seen them. I could see the dome formed by the Earth's atmosphere and the moon coming up over the distant hills. I just watched them, feeling completely connected and entertained by this deep beauty as I fell asleep.

Later the coyotes, even closer this time, woke me again, and as I looked up, I noticed how the stars had moved. Of course, I realized that the Earth had actually moved. The moon was in a different place, and the entire sky looked totally different. I had never actually watched the night sky change as I did that entire night. I could sense the movement and see changes I had never witnessed before.

I noticed that all the animals come out at night. I could see birds flying and creatures moving through the bush. The desert was alive and the colors were muted, not dark. I could see my shadow in the moonlight. I cannot describe the beauty and mystery I experienced that night.

In the morning I found myself laying on a rock watching the sun rise from behind some small hills. I watched as the colors changed and as the angle of the sun changed. Subtle shifts in brightness and width of color bands spread across the desert. The animals were hiding, except for a lizard who sat on the rock next to me watching the same sunrise. A totally different beauty played out in front of my eyes, again, beyond description.

For the rest of that day, and into the next, I felt more relaxed than I had ever felt before. There was no hurry or boredom. The desert was full of beauty. Some of the cactus had blossoms, and there was an eagles nest high up in the rocks over the camp. I could feel my wife's beautiful heart from the distance, and every step was full of joy. I had let go of all the thoughts that carried worries and was wandering in the moment. I felt as though I had returned to the Garden of Eden in a state free from the knowledge of good and evil, safe and ecstatic. The simplest things fascinated me and I felt totally free.

During the drive home, my wife and I were not even bothered by traffic, and were so full of stories and joy, that we missed our exit, but were thrilled to find a new place we had not seen before. This feeling lasted through the day, and to this day is an anchor for us. Through our experience, we touched the "Great Intelligence" and know that letting go of circular thought allows a life beyond description.

This is presence. It has a power and a level of attraction that great leaders find. A person who is in this state of mind has knowledge beyond their memories. I know, as native tribes have always known, I could have found water if I had needed it, because my senses were so sharp.

Presence is disarming. Imagine a conference room full of business people arguing over something they think is important, and then suddenly the door opens. A young woman with a new baby enters. All the stress leaves the room and everyone enjoys the baby who, of course, is totally present. A shift away from shallow circular thoughts occurs when someone is present. That is why it is critical for leaders to master being in the moment.

Like the stillness of the desert helped me let go of my ego and the thoughts that swirled around in my head, a leader with stillness will do the same for their team. I strongly suggest you spend time deep in nature where the stillness is unavoidable.

Meditation Technique

The following is a simple meditation technique that can help you find the stillness within yourself. It will help establish an inner road map to stillness, which allows the "Great Intelligence" to interact with you.

1. **The Right Environment:** Find a quiet place and arrange to have no distractions or interruptions. A special place in your home or a place out in nature. It is especially important in the first stages of meditation to

find a special place. It helps you move towards stillness naturally. Over time you will be able to meditate anywhere, at any time, even as you walk through hallways.

2. **Sit Comfortably:** You want your body to be at ease. Find a chair that is comfortable and sit up straight; be sure not to cross you arms or legs. Sitting up straight in a way that you will not have to move should one of your limbs fall asleep is important.

3. **Three Deep Breaths:** Take three deep breaths and hold the oxygen in as long as you can on each breath, and let the oxygen out suddenly once you can no longer hold the air.

4. **Breathe Normally:** Return to your normal breathing pattern. Close your eyes and put your attention on your breathing process. Follow your breath in and then out. Notice the rhythm and depth of each of your breaths. Spend 2–3 minutes just following your breath with your attention.

5. **Imagine a Beautiful Place:** Imagine yourself in a beautiful place in nature. Choose a favorite spot or create a spot that would be ideal for you. Each time you begin meditating come back to this place. It will serve as an anchor for peace and help you to relax each time. Once you have felt the peace of this place, use it as a background and return your attention to your breathing.

6. **Let Go of Thoughts:** As thoughts arise in your mind, do not resist them. Practice observing without processing,

and then letting go of them. You can imagine them floating up into the sky or being absorbed by nature. As you let go, return your attention to your breathing.

7. **Deepen Your Breathing:** Once you have found your natural rhythm increase the depth of your breathing. Inhale 10–15 percent deeper and exhale 10–15 percent deeper. Play with this deeper rhythm until it becomes natural. Continue to let go of thoughts as they arise.

8. **Notice Stillness:** Notice that at the moment you fully inhale, just before you exhale, there is a still point. Likewise, after you have fully exhaled, there is the same still point. The inhale, is full and the exhale, is empty. Notice the difference.

9. **Fall into Stillness:** At times when your total focus is on this deeper breathing process, you will notice the stillness inside you. Let your consciousness fall into this stillness. Let go and don't be afraid; it is your destination. Stay there as long as your ego will allow. It might take a number of sessions before you achieve this, but it is worth the practice and discipline.

10. **Open Your Eyes:** In about 20-25 minutes, gently open your eyes without moving and notice the world around you. Notice your state of mind and journal your experience.

11. **Take This State of Mind With You:** Practice staying with this state of mind as you get up from your chair and walk, focusing on your breathing as before. Find a rhythm between your steps and your breath. Count how many breaths per step until you find a comfortable pace

that is a little deeper than normal. This will help you begin to integrate this state of mind into your daily life.

12. **Do Short Meditations:** Once you have mastered this practice, you will be able to take a few minutes to clear your mind between meetings or even with short pauses during meetings.

Meditation creates the same state of being that Florence Joyner and other athletes achieve when they are in "The Zone." Your consciousness will deepen and widen and you will be able to perform more effectively. Remember, **there is no substitute for practice.**

As you continue to meditate, you will find the quality of your thought improving. You will have great ideas and find it easy to solve problems you are struggling with. Creating this space of stillness within yourself leaves room for the "Great Intelligence" to combine with your understanding. Meditation is a powerful tool for those who are creating the future. It helps with idea generation and stress reduction. If you are a leader, you need both to be successful.

Integrative Presence is achieved by:

- Understanding the present is the only true reality
- Letting go of the past
- Not worrying about the future
- Connecting with the reality of the moment
- Observing the future as it is born in the present
- Collaborating with the future as it evolves in the moment
- Practice techniques

COURAGE

"Our deepest fear is not that we are inadequate. Our deepest fear is that we are powerful beyond measure. It is our light, not our dark-ness, that most frightens us. We ask ourselves, who am I to be brilliant, to be gorgeous, talented, and fabulous. Actually, who are you not to be? You are a child of God. Your playing small doesn't serve the world. There is nothing enlightened about shrinking so that oth-ers won't feel insecure around you. We are born to make manifest the glory of God within us. It is not just in some of us, it is in everyone. And as we let our light shine, we consciously give others permission to do the same. As we are liberated from our own fear, our presence automatically liberates others."

—Marianne Williamson, "A Return to Love"

When I was working with Frank Mori, CEO of Anne Klein, in the 1980's, he told me a story that truly represents both courage and vision. An overseas investor had bought Anne Klein and asked him to become the CEO to turn this icon of the fashion industry into a truly excellent business. Three months after the purchase of the business, Anne

Klein, who was the chief designer and founder, suddenly died. It was a total disaster.

Everyone told Frank that the business was finished. How could a fashion business survive without the branded leader of the business? At the time, people were loyal to the designer, not the company. All that Frank had left was the two junior designers, Louis DellOlio and Donna Karen, who were both unknown.

The CEO spent many hours looking at various alternatives to revive or liquidate the business, and none of them were workable. Finally, after talking with the two designers, Frank decided to bet the entire company on the upcoming fall line, which had not been designed. He knew everyone would be watching. The whole industry was poised to report the failed attempt at professionalizing such a business, and talk about how there is no substitute for artistic leadership. They were already hinting that no "professional CEO" can run a fashion business.

In spite of all those who were predicting failure, Frank decided not only to go forward with the fall line but to rent the Winter Garden Theater, instead of showing the line, on 7th Avenue as usual. The Theater held many more people than the venues on 7th Avenue, and opening your fall line there had risks at multiple levels.

He sat down with Donna Karen and Louis DellOlio and explained that we are either going to go out of business or be an incredible success. He said, "Since I don't really know the business, it is up to both of you. Our fates are in your hands, but know that we will provide all the resources you need to succeed this fall." He went on to announce to the industry that the fall line would open at the Winter Garden Theater instead of 7th Avenue.

Imagine how Donna Karen and Louis DellOlio must have felt. They were both in their twenties and had never led a fashion show of this kind. They worked hard on the line and the show. The theater was full that night of the fashion elite and the press. The show opened and finished with seven standing ovations. It was a tremendous success. The courage Frank, Louis and Donna displayed changed the energy from certain failure to success. All learned the lesson of Marianne Williamson's words:

"It is our light, not our darkness, that most frightens us. We ask ourselves, who am I to be brilliant, to be gorgeous, talented, and fabulous. Actually, who are you not to be?"

Anne Klein grew to be one of the largest fashion houses in New York City, diversified their lines and is still a strong brand today. Louis DellOlio and Donna Karen went on to success in their own right. Donna Karen started her own firm, and Louis went on to be the lead designer of Anne Klein. There was vision, strong intention, commitment and creativity. This example is of a dramatic event, but this kind of courage is required of a leader every day.

Being Connected to Reality

When a leader demonstrates courage, people jump in with their support, and the human spirit takes vertical leaps. Don Ross of New York Life was very courageous when he resisted the pressure of most of the people in his company. They wanted him to stop moving money out of the stock market. They were accusing him of being old and foolish, suggesting it was time for him to take an early retirement. But as he said to me, "I just knew." This knowing is the source of courage.

Being connected with "The Great Intelligence" by having a still mind in the storms of the business world enables clarity of thought. It is the source of true intention which drives courage. Lord Nelson, as he stood on the deck of his ship Victory, had a knowing and confidence that led his sailors into the largest naval battle in history. I was not there, but I can imagine how still he was as he sailed into the combined French and Spanish fleet. Cannon balls flying at his ship from both sides as he led his fleet into the center of a larger enemy force. He could not have done this without great courage, which always comes from a deep knowing.

The courage Nelson displayed in previous battles caused his sailors and all of England to give him unconditional support, as did those at New York Life once they saw the wisdom and courage that Don Ross displayed. A leader who displays courage draws out the spirit and courage in others. There are many tales of this kind of courage, but the following story was told to me by my mother and father about their experience during World War II in England.

Facing Evil

After the battle of Dunkirk in 1940, the British Army was in retreat and the spirit of Britain was deflated. Nearly all the British arms were left in France after a hasty retreat that was only completed with the help of fishing and pleasure boats from across the English Channel. Britain's defenses were crippled. Hitler could have easily taken control of London by sending armored boats up the Thames. The British people were dispirited, until the evening Winston Churchill delivered his now famous "Blood, Sweat and Tears" speech.

Battered and humiliated, Britain was the lone European survivor of the Nazi war machine. All others had been crushed or surrendered. The consensus opinion was that there was little chance of success against the Germans. It was time to compromise, to capitulate to a superior force. A "manager" would have made a deal; but not a leader. On the brink of the worst defeat in the history of the British Empire, Winston Churchill stood up and said, "We will never surrender."

The stakes were high. Hitler's Nazis were murdering millions of people for much lower levels of resistance. Churchill stepped beyond the point of no return. He put his career, his honor and, most certainly, his life, on the line. Hitler would have surely made an example of him after defeat. He would have crucified him in some way in Trafalgar Square, filmed and written it into history. The British people could have turned on Churchill because he was also committing their lives. But Churchill never wavered. He proclaimed the British would fight on the beaches and in the streets until the last drop of blood was spilled.

He called back the spirit of the British people and captured the imagination of the rest of the free world. He invoked the spirit of Arthur, William Wallace, Lord Nelson at Trafalgar, and of the great Kings. He called back the spirit of Queen Elizabeth I who seemed to summon up nature itself to defeat the Spanish Armada in 1588. He called back the spirit of Britannia and of the Celt's who resisted the Roman invaders. He created a force larger than life. The desire for, as William Wallace said, as he was being disemboweled, "Freedom." The human spirit was strong that morning. It loomed over the British Isles like an enormous dome of light washing away the strength of the dark forces that waited on the shores of Europe.

My dad and mom, like everyone else, huddled around the radio to hear Winston Churchill's speech. It could have been careful and safe. It was not! Though people were fearful, it connected them with truth and light. It was, and is today, a compelling example of leadership at its greatest. My mom and dad said that Britain was a different country after that speech. People found their courage and joined the Civil Defense, turned in any steel they could find to be melted down into weapons, and prepared themselves with hunting rifles and pistols. They found the courage to follow their leader, to stand firm in the face of a terrible dark adversity.

This single moment of courage changed the course of World War II and the direction of modern civilization. It was one of many courageous stands for freedom vs. tyranny. Courage expands the human spirit and creates an energy field that is powerful. Great Britain stood strong that night and the entire world saw the truth that the courage was defending. The United States had not yet entered the war, and this moment of courage drew them to Britain's and freedom's side.

The immensity of this energy that emanated from Britain made the German war machine hesitate. It is a lot easier to roll your armies and tanks over a nation that lacks true courage. Fighting a people who are connected to a cause that is conceived in wisdom and truth is much more difficult. You are not only fighting people and weapons; you are fighting a deep spiritual presence. The Nazi's were not fighting a nation; they were fighting the truth of the deep and innate desire of people to live in freedom.

True courage and power is connected to goodness and truth. Anger and hatred can create a force that tramples over peoples' spirit and holds them prisoner for a time, because people are fearful when separated from the truth and the light. But no matter how powerful the forces of darkness and destruction are, eventually true courage connected with "The Great Intelligence," and the light that emanates from that intelligence, emerges.

Fear Does Not Work

A leader must be careful not to get seduced by strategies based on using fear to dominate people. It is a shortcut and will never achieve true power. The practice of using fear to dominate your team and company is as inferior as the Nazi's were, once the world connected with their true desires for freedom. Metaphorically, you will go down with a gun in your mouth hidden away underground in a bunker, just as Hitler did as his dark empire fell all around him.

Leaders have power by the virtue of their position and resources at their disposal. Using this power to create obedience based on fear will work in the short term, but will fail in the long term. In a business, truly good and powerful people will leave you, and you will only be left with people who are driven by fear. They will tell you what you want to hear for fear of your wrath. This will feed your ego but seal you off from their wisdom and insight. You will begin to feel alone and disrespected even though no one will really speak up. You will find yourself surrounded by broken people who you have pushed down, and they will become a millstone around your neck.

Their unexpressed hatred and resentment will suck the energy out of you and stimulate your anger which will start the cycle of abuse. Your family will eventually sense the darkness around you, and they too will run. Make no mistake about it, the path of intimidation and fear will lead to an ugly fall eventually. It may not be today or even this year, but it will come. It may not be obvious at first, but it will begin with stress inside you and start to tear you down as a person. There will be stress-related illnesses and disloyalties from employees inside your team.

The word will find its way into your industry and market place and, when you walk into a meeting, you will be able to sense the subtle looks of disapproval. People will talk behind your back, and your only friends will be the people who depend on you for their livelihood or hope to gain favor from their relationship with you. You will be surrounded by takers who are a mirror of who you have become.

If you are in this cycle, I strongly recommend you stop now. Take advice from one of the early leadership coaches, Lao Tzu:

"The mystical techniques for achieving immortality are revealed only to those who have dissolved all ties to the gross worldly realm of duality, conflict, and dogma. As long as your shallow worldly ambitions exist, the door will not open."—The Hua Hu Ching

Learn to be a leader who releases the human spirit by connecting with truth and wisdom. It is never too late. Churchill could have capitulated and compromised with

Hitler. It was the easiest course of action. But imagine how different his legacy and life would have been. There is always an opportunity for forgiveness. People will forgive if they see you are sincere in your repentance. In fact, your role model of transformation can be a powerful force.

Sometimes, it is just too late. A company can be destroyed beyond repair. Hitler's huge mistake of instilling such a high level of fear within his commanding ranks caused them to make poor strategic decisions because they feared Hitler more than defeat. Their attention was wasted on appeasing their leader, rather than fighting a world war. Hitler was left in the dark, intel-wise, because nobody would tell him the bad news, or offer alternative input, thus forcing him to make fatal strategic decisions.

Going back to the battle of Dunkirk, we find an example of the weakness of a leader who rules by fear. Historians always wondered why the Nazi's did not attack the British troops once they were trapped on the French shores. Their armies stood idle for three days and allowed time for the British troops to escape across the English Channel. As scholars began to study the war, they found that Hitler was in his mountain retreat with his mistress, and no one could reach him. The Nazi command would not dare launch a major offensive without Hitler's direct approval. The result of this kind of fear-based leadership was the entire British army escaped, which emboldened Great Britain. Trust once lost is hard to regain, but if you start to follow the practices in this book you will learn to build trust. People will see the change and you will start attracting truly powerful people. If your spirits have not been totally destroyed you may rise up out of your darkness and start to feel good about yourself.

Connect to Wisdom

Of course, it takes courage. Remember, that courage comes when you are connected with wisdom and light, when you tame your ego and fear and combine your knowledge with "The Great Intelligence." As Marianne Williamson said:

"And as we let our light shine, we consciously give others permission to do the same. As we are liberated from our own fear, our presence automatically liberates others."

Great leaders have the courage to act once they have connected with wisdom, and those actions create chain reactions that can change the world. Buddha was the first in India to allow untouchables into the priesthood. He knew they had the light inside like any other person and acted on his deep understanding. Christ new the Kingdom of Heaven was in each of us, and so forgave his persecutors from the cross. The founding fathers of the United States knew that "All men are created equal and have the right to life, liberty and the pursuit of happiness." They created ideas that still attract people from all over the world today.

Discover your truth and connect to your destiny. Commit the time and discipline to find your road map to the wisdom within you. Nothing is more important. Become an enormous dome of light as Winston Churchill did. Build a company that people will tell stories about decades from now. Build a company that people tell their families and friends about. Create new realities that transform our world. It takes courage. You will be fearful, and lesser people will try to drag you down with sinister beliefs and darkness, but take a stand before it is too late. Create a future that changes the course of your world.

Keys to creating courage in yourself and others:
- Being connected to the reality of the present
- Evil and the dragons of darkness will challenge every leader; like a mythical Knight, you must kill those dragons
- Leading people with fear does not draw out their courage, it sends them underground
- Connecting to wisdom and people's dreams unleashes courage
- The leader, once the mission is discovered, must be the guardian and champion

SUMMARY

"He who is not busy being born, is busy dying.."

—*Bob Dylan*

If your team, family or company is not expanding, then as Bob Dylan implies by his quote, it is contracting. I have written this book to help leaders of all kinds develop the knowledge and courage to create new realities in leadership. I would like to see a world of leaders who are committed to unleashing their genius and the genius of their teams.

If you want to lead a team of business leaders to a series of championships, I am passionate about using my experience to help, but I warn you now that it will not be easy. One of my leaders, after explaining that I had helped him achieve his dream said, "I was constantly learning, but it was the hardest thing I have ever done." It takes courage, compassion, humility, wisdom, an ability to conceive the future, and many other things. It is not a job for the weak at heart. Without this understanding, I have seen good men broken; leaders who have lost their families and confidence, and others who turned bitter and cynical.

However, with this understanding, the feeling of walking into a room full of gratitude and warmth at the end of a winning year, knowing you were part of the leadership, is a feeling beyond description. To see a team committed to something larger than themselves and to each other, telling stories of their wins and dancing with their children in the glow of gratitude, can last a lifetime. Knowing that you have made a big difference in the lives of people, and helped them discover parts of themselves that will enrich their lives, is sweet. It is a rare prize worth all the work.

As a leader, your biggest challenge is doing what you know, not knowing what to do. It is not finding the right strategy; it is getting people to follow the right strategy. The challenge is humanity itself. All championship teams are carved out of society at large, and most societies are full of selfishness and mediocrity. The world at large is not nearly a championship team, but as a leader you must develop and maintain the people on your team against the tide of a floundering world. There will be dragons to slay within your team, in your markets and within yourself.

As a leader, you must know yourself at the deepest level to prevent the world around you from dragging you down, and you must understand human thought and behavior to turn people around or select the right players. The final decision will come to you. You must be armed with knowledge, humility, wisdom and courage. At the same time it is essential that you do not take yourself too seriously; if you do, the weight of your ego will crush you.

To create a team that is continuously expanding themselves, their business and their world, and to create something better, thereby extending the universe that has been given to us, is in my view, the purpose of life. Leaders that build organizations that contribute to the lives of the people that follow them, their families, their communities and the world, are special people. They lead a complex creative process that can discover new realities in human ability and potential. It is my honor to be a trusted advisor, coach and consultant to those who choose to lead.

When we think we have discovered new ideas, we find that philosophers for thousands of years have been trying to tell us these things. This ancient Taoist riddle that I presented to you in the introduction sums up much of what I have been talking about.

"First there is a Mountain, then there is no Mountain, then there is." -Taoist Riddle

First there is a mountain	Then there is no mountain	Then there is
A child knows few concepts and sees the mountain as it is	As adults, we must master concepts & beliefs, thus losing sight of the mountain	Then the true journey begins When we awaken from the illusion of concept, again we see the mountain, but now we will never go back

Attachment to concepts and beliefs can separate you from life itself.

The mountain is a metaphor for seeing the truth. As a child we see the world as it is without the distortion of comparative thought. "First there is a mountain..."

But in order to live in this world, we must learn to master concept and thought. During this process, we make the mistake of thinking thought itself is reality. We lose sight of the mountain trying to navigate through the world. Trying to create our place in the matrix of thought that defines this world, we become lost. We think it is real and feel emptiness. It is as though we are eating the menu instead of the food on the menu. "Then there is no mountain..."

When we reconnect with "The Great Intelligence" through "Integrative Presence" and begin to live more connected with reality, then we are, as Jesus said, "Reborn." The Buddha said, "Awakened." Others use the word "Enlightened." We see the mountain again. We can view reality without the distortion of thought. We can still use thought to create, but it no longer imprisons us and blinds us to the mountain. "Then there is."

The difference between this third state and the state of innocence a child experiences is that after awakening, it is more difficult to become corrupted and lost. You know the state of mind that is closer to reality and you also know the previous state of mind you experienced when you were lost in cognitive distortion. That state of mind begins to feel very uncomfortable. You begin to seek deeper levels of awakening, and continue to move away from the shadowy state of mind that is defined by concept and belief.

The exciting part about this for a business leader is that insight into present reality is the best tool for creating new realities. The blessing for all of us was explained to me by a man that lives most often in this state of awakening. Sydney Banks, who was literally glowing, leaned over and looked into my eyes and said, "Paul, I want you to know that there is no limit to the depth of this understanding. Like the Universe, you can expand infinitely. I discover more each day. Once you truly begin this journey, it is an endless dance of joy and discovery."

I hope this book has helped you create a compelling picture of the possibility that waits for you to discover. I hope you become committed to achieving new realities in your life. I hope your leaders learn how to communicate, acknowledge reality, create plans, take decisive actions and develop feedback systems to be sure you stay on track.

But most of all, I hope that you are feeling more comfortable living in "Integrative Presence," having discovered how to unleash the genius within yourself. Because, with that knowledge, you will be able to help others unleash their genius, and build teams of people who work together synchronizing their genius to create new realities for our world. With work, you can create new realities in leadership for your organization, your family, your country, and yourself.

As we have learned from Einstein, Dylan, and others, intention is much more than a wish or a vision; it is a connection from the present with a series of flows that are extending into the future. You can experience, and connect with, a pattern of unfolding events, and by that connection, accelerate them. Your presence can organize streams of events and synchronize with them almost as though you are riding the winds of change. It is collaboration with destiny itself.

Please make your engagement with this book collaboration with your destiny. Don't get lost in fixed thoughts and ideas while your true destiny passes you by. Go back over your insights and actions in your journal. Review and rewrite them summarizing each insight. Work each day to unleash yourself from illusions, and find your roadmap to your genius. Discuss your insights with others and notice their responses, as you do, practice and journal, be open to insight. Hold an intention that will let you discover your genius in moments of insight. It will come to you. It is already there.

Remember: There is no Substitute for Practice

If you have not written insights and action steps your journal please do it now. You can also join us on our website at www.pauldavidwalker.com for practice and dialogues with other leaders, and when you are ready, join our Leadership Institute.

Remember:

- Unleashing Genius takes courage, presence, insight, commitment, powerful vision, expansion, being connected, mastery of thought, connecting with wisdom, and a passion to create new realities in the world
- It is not easy, but worth the work
- Remember, if you are not expanding, you are contracting

ABOUT THE AUTHOR

Paul is a CEO Coach and was one of the early innovators of leadership consulting and coaching at the executive level. He has been advising the leaders of Fortune 500 and midsized companies for over twenty-five years. With this experience, he brings a unique perspective that can be invaluable to leaders. Paul has advised leaders through three downturns and recoveries in the economy. He has lead turnarounds, acquisition integration, rapid growth, culture change and strategic projects to align strategy, structure and culture. He has coached and mentored leaders in the art of leadership, personal balance, and philosophical understandings that have helped his clients manifest innovative ideas. He is known to be someone who sees and draws out the genius in leaders.

While advising and coaching Fortune 500 companies, he was one of the leaders of a groundbreaking entrepreneurial company that established innovative leadership consulting practices. These practices provided the foundation for much of the leadership consulting that exists today. Still on the leading edge of business consulting, he integrates new approaches from science, psychology and philosophy, while bringing concrete business acumen.

He will involve you in an explorative dialogue that will expand your understanding of how to extend present reality into a successful future. Your understanding of leadership, yourself and your business will take a quantum leap.

Paul is a master storyteller, using humor and insight to stimulate learning from the day-to-day experience of leading a business. He asks his clients to tell and analyze their greatest success stories to create a "line of sight" to their genius. Leadership teams, while laughing and creating self-knowledge, bond together to win.

What Makes Paul Unique

Paul is a rugged man who is comfortable leading teams on white water journeys, coaching an Executive team, and reading poetry from his books, Storms and Clearings and A Glimpse. He is a force of nature. With his 25 years of experience consulting and coaching CEO's, he understands what it takes to lead Fortune 500 and midsized companies, and yet he is able to inspire his neighbors to unleash their genius.

Paul has a strong following of leaders, and those who coach leaders, and is one of the founders of the executive leadership coaching movement in America. He is a classic American success story who was raised on a small farm in Michigan and worked his way to the top of the leadership consulting profession. He has a great sense of humor, is humble, inspiring, and charms everyone he meets. His book Unleashing Genius is the result of hundreds of clients and friends insisting he capture his unique wisdom in writing. It is deeply profound, while being grounded in common sense, and is written in a poetic fashion that draws out people's deepest yearnings.

Paul David Walker...

- A classic American success story who rose from a farm to Fortune 500 board rooms coaching CEO's and their teams
- Twenty-five years of CEO and executive leadership consulting and coaching vs. academic studies and theories
- Translates deep philosophical understandings in a way that every person understands vs. psychology and "new models"
- Unleashes existing genius found within each person and company vs. the latest theories and models
- Committed to making leadership a noble and respected profession vs. present tainted brand
- Great storyteller and speaker who effectively intertwines these real life company and personality stories with powerful personal presence
- A poet and philosopher

A Gift for You
from Paul David Walker!

*In this insightful Bonus DVD,
Paul David Walker sheds light
on the true essence of genius.*

Simply log-on to:
www.pauldavidwalker.com/bonusDVD
to view or download this amazing DVD.

Printed in the USA
CPSIA information can be obtained
at www.ICGtesting.com
JSHW082203140824
68134JS00014B/401